CONTENTS

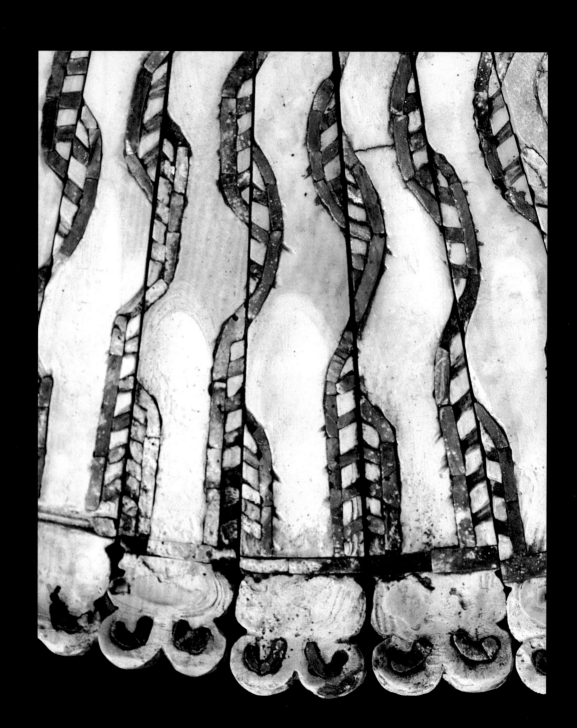

ACKNOWLEDGMENTS

▼ *Royal Tombs of Sipán* has been an unusually complex project. The excavation, conservation and exhibition of the Sipán tomb contents, as well as the publication of this volume, has involved the close collaboration of many individuals and institutions in Peru, Germany, and the United States — each working on a different aspect of the project to create an integrated whole. It has proven to be a model of international scientific teamwork, thanks to the generosity, talent, and dedication of the various individuals and institutions involved.

Primary support for the Royal Tombs of Sipán exhibition and this catalogue was provided by the National Endowment for the Humanities and the Ahmanson Foundation. Further support was provided by an indemnity from the Federal Council on the Arts and Humanities, the Ethnic Arts Council of Los Angeles, Varig Airlines, the Times-Mirror Foundation, and Manus, the support group of the Fowler Museum of Cultural History.

The excavation of the Sipán tombs was made possible by funds provided by the National Geographic Society, the H. John Heinz III Charitable Trust, Patronato de Cultura de Lambayeque, Cervecería del Norte, Corporación Departamental de Lambayeque, and recently, the Sociedad Estatal del Quinto Centenario, España. Individuals associated with these institutions who were particularly helpful include Robert Hernandez, Betty Meggers, George Stuart, William D. Perry, Jr., James Richardson III, Georgio Batistini, Juan Brescia, and Guillermo Baca. Various types of support for constructing the field station, site museum, and conservation laboratory were provided by the Oficina de Apoyo Alimentario, Eternit del Perú S.A., Volkswagen del Perú, and Sallbgittes GMB, the Banco de Reconstrucción de Alemania, Banco Latino, Banco Wiese Ltdo., Banco Crédito, Banco Mercantil, y Fondo de Promoción Turistica del Perú. Luis Chero, resident archaeologist, and Susana Meneses were in charge of the field investigations. They deserve special recognition; results of their work are in this book.

We are grateful to the Policía Nacional del Perú for its help in recovering looted material from Sipán, and for providing security both at the Sipán excavation and at the Museo Nacional Bruning de Lambayeque, Perú. Special thanks are due to General Carlos Ruiz Mondragón and General Edilberto Temoche.

Conservation of part of the Sipán objects was carried out by the Römisch-Germanisches Zentralmuseum in Mainz, Germany, directed by Konrad Weidemann. It resulted from initial coordination by Michael Tellenbach. Peter Schauer, Christian Eckmann, and Maiken Fecht were responsible for the success of this work. Conservation of other Sipán objects was carried out at the Bruning Museum by Fidel V. Gutiérrez, Félix V. Gutiérrez, Ramón G. Morante, Segundo R. González, Ethel D. Oblitas, and Johnny G. Aldana. This laboratory is supported with the help of Corporación Backus y Johnston S.A., thanks to the personal involvement of Carlos and Elías Bentín.

All of the Sipán objects in the exhibition were provided by the Bruning Museum in Lambayeque. They were augmented by Moche objects from the collection of the Fowler Museum of Cultural History. We are grateful to the following individuals who facilitated loans from two other institutions— María del Pilar Remy, Pedro Pablo Alayza, and Hermilio Rosas of the Museo Nacional de Arqueología, Antropología e Historia del Peru in Lima, and to Helmut Schindler, Maria Kecskési and Walter Raunig of the Statliches Museum für Völkerkunde in Munich.

Other individuals who deserve special recognition for their part in making this exhibition and catalogue a reality are Franklin Pease, Mariana Mould de Pease, Jorge Cock, Patricia Días, Guillermo Hare, Jaime Arrieta, Carmela Zanelli, Luis Jaime Castillo, Richard Chute, Lorna Profant, Mary E. Doyle, Alana Cordy-Collins, Geraldine Ford and Marsha Semmel.

Herbert Lucas, Lloyd Cotsen, and Franklin Murphy took a personal interest in this exhibition, and were instrumental in generating support for its related public programming. Also helpful in this regard were Miguel Angel Corzo, David Scott, and Neville Agnew of the Getty Conservation Institute, Tom Reese of the Getty Center for the History of Art and the Humanities, and Lee Walcott and the Board of Directors of The Ahmanson Foundation.

The employees of the Bruning Museum and the Fowler Museum of Cultural History worked tirelessly to complete each aspect of the exhibition and publication on schedule, and did so with extraordinary skill and dedication. At the Bruning Museum, Flor Wong, Leonardo Córdova, and Benedicto Rodriguez provided skillful administrative assistance and logistics, while Carlos Wester, José Centurión, and Juan Martínez carried out a variety of photographic, inventory, and shipping arrangements. Two skilled artists at the Bruning Museum, Alberto Gutierrez and Percy Fiestas, produced most of the oil paintings and pen and ink drawings that enhance the exhibition and catalogue. Susana Meneses participated in all stages of planning the exhibition. Her assistance throughout this project is profoundly appreciated.

The exhibition was designed by David Mayo, and installed in the J. Paul Getty Trust Gallery at the Fowler Museum of Cultural History by Gene Riggs, Don Simmons, Victor Lozano and Patrick White. Robin Chamberlin Milburn monitored the condition of the objects, while their insurance and transportation were dealt with by Sarah Kennington, Cynthia Eckholm, Owen Moore, and Fran Tabbush. Denis Nervig assisted with photography, Guillermo Cock and Bobby Whitaker were responsible for museum security, and Polly Svenson, Sue Kallick, and Marilyn Liebman coordinated the Museum Store. Betsy Quick, in collaboration with the Los Angeles Unified School District, developed the educational program for elementary and secondary school visits. Christine Sellin, Kay Sanger, and Debbie Last publicized the exhibition and developed related events. Millicent Besser, with the able assistance of Daniel Shen and Arthur Bond, dealt with the complex financial accounting, Betsy Escandor and Cristina de la Torre provided secretarial assistance, and Barbara Underwood provided critical administrative support. The production of this volume was done by four very talented individuals: Barbara Kelly, Judy Hale, Daniel R. Brauer, and Anthony A.G. Kluck.

Special gratitude goes to Doran H. Ross, Deputy Director of the Fowler Museum, Vice Chancellor Richard Sisson, Vice Chancellor (Emeritus) Elwin Svenson, and Executive Officer Connie Chittick for their consistent support of Royal Tombs of Sipán, and to Chancellor Charles Young for having the vision to create a university museum that could produce an exhibit of this significance.

There are three individuals whose assistance was so critical throughout the development of both the exhibition and publication that it is impossible to imagine how either could have been accomplished without them. They are Donna and Don McClelland and Guillermo Cock. Each had an unwavering belief in this project, and we are profoundly grateful for the skill, dedication, wisdom and countless hours that they devoted to making Royal Tombs of Sipán a reality. Whatever success it has is due to their involvement.

Finally, we wish to acknowledge the critical support provided by various individuals and institutions of the Peruvian government. The Instituto Nacional de Cultura in Perú has consistently given its enthusiastic endorsement and full cooperation for the excavation and conservation of the Sipán tomb contents, as well as for this exhibition. Their support began under two former directors, Germán Peralta and Elías Mujica, and has continued to develop under the present Director, Pedro Gjurinovic. Alberto Varillas, Minister of Education, has provided his valuable advice and strong support for this exhibition. Above all, we are grateful to the President of Perú, Alberto Fujimori, for authorizing the loan of the Sipán treasures. We greatly appreciate his confidence in this exhibition, and his belief that it will create a wonderful opportunity for people in the United States to experience the remarkable cultural heritage of Peru.

PREFACE

▼ *Royal Tombs of Sipán* was written to serve as a catalogue for the museum exhibition of the same name. Its primary aim is to provide an account of the discovery, excavation,[1] and current interpretation of the three royal tombs that were scientifically recovered from Sipán between 1987 and 1990. We have tried to relate them to the royal tomb that, so tragically, was looted at Sipán before the archaeological work began, and to demonstrate the value of careful archaeological excavation as opposed to clandestine looting.

Although it is hoped that the detailed accounts of the tombs provided here will be useful for scholars, the volume was written primarily for the non-specialist. The story is presented in narrative form, often using phrases like "we found," "we thought," or "we realized." The reader might infer from this that "we" means simply the authors. But the team was much larger than the authors of this volume, and both responsibility and primary involvement in distinct aspects of the work were often divided. Walter Alva was the archaeologist who directed the excavations at Sipán, assisted by archaeologists Luis Chero and Susana Meneses. Working with a wonderful team of archaeology students from The Universidad Nacional de Trujillo, they discovered all three of the royal tombs at Sipán, and saw to it that each was documented in an exemplary fashion.

Christopher Donnan was at Sipán to witness most of the major stages in the excavation, and to discuss the interpretation of the tombs and their contents with the Peruvian archaeologists who excavated them. His primary role was the iconographic analysis — identifying the tombs' objects and individuals by comparisons with their representation in Moche art, and relating the tombs and their contents to specific aspects of Moche culture. Much of this work was done in the Moche Archive at the University of California in Los Angeles, and involved close collaboration with his research associate, Donna McClelland.

Although a great deal more has been excavated at Sipán than the three tombs reported in this volume, those materials will be published at a later date by the archaeologists who were involved in their excavation. Moreover, a much more detailed account of the royal tombs is now in preparation. It will provide the numerous plans and profiles that were made of each aspect of the excavation, together with the results of analyses by botanists, zoologists, metallurgists, and textile analysts who are currently working with the tomb contents.

---

[1] Throughout this book, the term "excavation" will be used to signify the careful scientific process of uncovering and removing objects from archaeological sites.

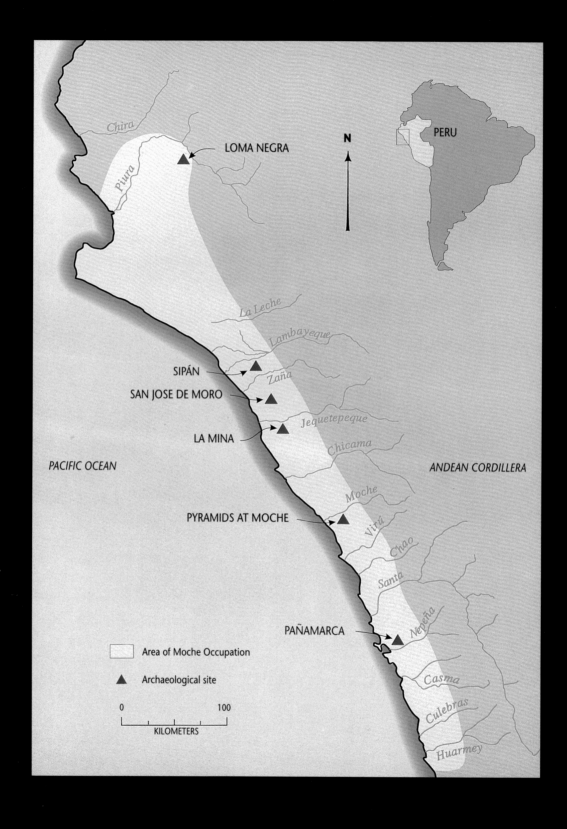

LOMA NEGRA

Chira

Piura

PERU

N

PACIFIC OCEAN

La Leche

Lambayeque

SIPÁN

Zaña

SAN JOSE DE MORO

LA MINA

Jequetepeque

Chicama

ANDEAN CORDILLERA

Moche

PYRAMIDS AT MOCHE

Virú

Chao

Santa

PAÑAMARCA

Nepeña

☐ Area of Moche Occupation

▲ Archaeological site

Casma

Culebras

0   100

KILOMETERS

Huarmey

FIG. 1

———

*Map of the
north coast
of Peru.*

1 THE MOCHE OF ANCIENT PERU

▼ The Moche kingdom flourished on the arid coastal plain of northern Peru between the first and the eighth centuries A.D. Human occupation in this area was limited to a series of valleys whose rivers flow out of the Andean mountains toward the Pacific shore (Fig. 1). Archaeologists have traced the human occupation of this arid environment from the end of the Pleistocene, around 10,000 B.C., through the development of settled village farming communities, and the subsequent rise and fall of civilizations that took place prior to the arrival of Europeans in the sixteenth century.

Centuries before Moche civilization began, this coastal plain was occupied by cultures possessing monumental architecture, highly stratified societies, and sophisticated weaving, ceramics, and metallurgy. But the Moche took the arts, technology and social organization they had inherited from previous civilizations and developed them to form their own distinctive culture. In so doing, they created one of the most remarkable civilizations of the ancient world.

By channeling the rivers into a complex network of irrigation canals, the Moche greatly extended the land under cultivation, and thus supported abundant agriculture. They grew a wide variety of crops, including corn, beans, guava, avocados, squash, chili peppers, and peanuts. From the Pacific Ocean, as well as from rivers, marshes, and lagoons, they harvested a rich catch of fish, shrimp, crabs, crayfish, and mollusks. Domesticated llamas, guinea pigs, and ducks were additional sources of food, along with other animals, birds, snails, and wild plant foods which were occasionally hunted or gathered.

With an abundant and nutritious diet, the Moche sustained a dense, highly stratified population, which was able to devote large numbers of workers to the construction and maintenance of irrigation canal systems, pyramids, palaces, and temples.

The Moche kingdom was not large. At their greatest period of influence, the Moche occupied only the valleys from Piura to Huarmey, a distance of approximately 550 kilometers north-south. The east-west extent of the kingdom was considerably smaller. Their settlements are found only between the ocean shoreline and the point where the valley floodplains narrow as they enter the canyons leading up into the Andean mountain range — a distance of generally about fifty to eighty kilometers.

Yet the Moche maintained trade relationships with people living far beyond the borders of their kingdom. They obtained lapis lazuli from hundreds of miles to the south, in what is now Chile. From hundreds of miles to the north, in what is now Ecuador, they acquired spondylus shells for ornaments as well as the boa constrictors, parrots, toucans, and monkeys that are so accurately portrayed in their art.

FIG. 2

*The Pyramid
of the Sun
at Moche.*

As one travels through the north coast of Peru today, the mud-brick pyramids are the most visible evidence of the Moche. They rise dramatically out of the agricultural fields or loom like large hills along the barren slopes that flank the verdant floodplains. The massive Pyramid of the Sun near the present-day city of Trujillo was the largest structure ever built in South America (Fig. 2). With a ramp that led up to small buildings at its flat summit, it stood approximately twenty-eight meters high, and sprawled over five hectares at its base. It once contained more than 130 million sun-dried mud bricks.

The Moche probably did not have markets or money, but they almost certainly practiced the system of redistribution characteristic of Andean people at the time of European contact. Local lords received from their subjects food and commodities which they subsequently distributed to nobles of lesser rank. In this way, vast quantities of raw materials and handmade goods were systematically collected and redistributed in an efficient manner.

The surplus from redistribution supported a corps of full-time artisans who created objects for the elite. Many of these items were used by the lords to demonstrate their power and wealth; others were given by them to lesser nobility to maintain social and political allegiances. With skilled craft specialists supported in this way, an ideal climate was created to stimulate artistic excellence and innovate sophisticated technology.

Moche potters were consummate masters of three-dimensional sculpture. In clay, they brought animals, plants, and anthropomorphic deities to life (Figs. 3, 4, 5). They depicted hunting and fish-

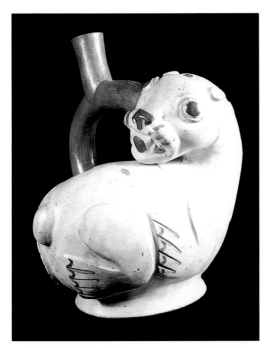

FIG. 3
—
(top left)
Sea lion.
H. 18.7 cms.

FIG. 4
—
(bottom)
Warty squash.
H. 24.3 cms.

FIG. 5
—
(top right)
Owl deity.
H. 27 cms.

FIG. 6

Portrait head jar.
H. 26.5 cms.

FIG. 7

Portrait head bottle.
H. 29 cms.

ing activities, mountain tableaux, rituals of combat, and elaborate ceremonies. Representations ranged from the pomp and power of enthroned rulers to depictions of the maimed and the blind.

Moche potters were able to skillfully capture the facial features of specific individuals in clay and to instill in each portrait a lifelike quality, rich in the subtle nuances of individual personality (Figs. 6, 7, 8). These portraits allow us to meet Moche people who lived more than 1500 years ago, and to sense something of their personal qualities.

FIG. 8

Portrait head bottle.
H. 35.6 cms.

FIG. 9
———
(top left)
Press molded
bottle with low
relief parrots.
H. 20.4 cms.

FIG. 10
———
(top right)
Bottle with
fineline painting
of musicians.
H. 26.2 cms.

FIG. 11
———
(below)
Drawing painted
on the chamber of
the bottle shown
in Figure 10.

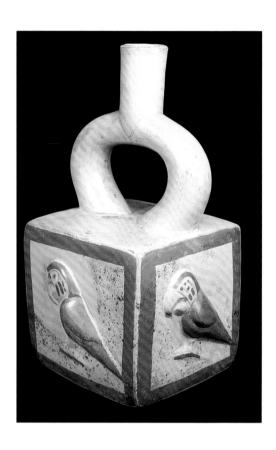

In addition to three-dimensional sculpture, Moche potters were skilled at decorating vessels with low relief designs (Fig. 9). Among the most intricate of these are scenes of skeletonized dancers holding hands in long processions, to the accompaniment of skeletonized musicians.

Like Greek vase painters of ancient Athens, Moche potters developed a technique for painting complex scenes on ceramic vessels. Through time, Moche vase painters became increasingly skillful at depicting intricate and lively scenes, many with multiple figures engaged in activities such as hunting, combat, and the enactment of elaborate ceremonies (Figs. 10, 11).

One of the Moche potters' most important technological innovations was the use of molds and stamps to produce ceramics quickly and efficiently (Fig. 12). By pressing moist clay into two halves of a mold, they were able to create an object much more rapidly than by hand modeling each piece. In a similar manner, the use of stamps greatly facilitated the decoration of ceramic vessels with low relief designs.

Molds and stamps were innovated early in Moche culture, and through time both became increasingly important in ceramic production. This resulted in numerous duplicates of individual pieces. Ultimately, elaborate ceramics became available to nearly all classes of people, and therefore were ineffective for demonstrating the power, wealth, and social status of the upper class.

In contrast, metal objects, particularly those of gold and silver, implied high status in the earliest Moche periods, and continued to be the exclusive property of the elite, not only throughout the span of Moche civilization, but in all subsequent civilizations that developed in the Andean area.

When the Spanish invaded Peru in the sixteenth century, they marveled at the sophistication and beauty of the gold and silver objects produced by Inca artisans. They noted that the metalworkers did not use bellows to create a forced draft of air in their furnaces, but instead blew into the coals with long tubes. A unique bowl (Fig. 13) shows that the Moche used similar blowtubes in their metalworking more than a thousand years earlier.

FIG. 12

(left) Mold for producing a ceramic figurine. H. 15.5 cms.

FIG. 13

(right) Metalworking with blowtubes. Dia. 29 cms.

FIG. 14

Gold and turquoise bead with lizard design. H. 4.5 cms.

Moche metalworkers were extremely sophisticated in the alloying of metals, using gold, silver, and copper in various combinations. With faceted stone hammers they then flattened and smoothed the metal into even sheets, which they shaped into low relief and three-dimensional sculpture (Fig. 14). They used solid metal forms (Fig. 15) over which sheet metal could be hammered to create sophisticated sculpture (Figs. 16a, b). Moche metalworkers excelled at joining metal pieces by edge-welding, soldering, crimping, and the use of tabs that projected through slits on adjacent pieces. Metalworkers were also skilled at lost wax casting. With this technique, they created complex three-dimensional sculptures, some of which have interlocking moveable parts.

These artisans developed ingenious techniques for making metal objects appear to be pure gold. One method was to fabricate the object from an alloy of gold and copper, or gold, copper, and silver, and then treat the surface chemically to remove the copper and silver, leaving the gold in place. Subsequent heating of the object would cause the surface gold to smooth out over the whole exterior, giving the object the appearance of solid gold (Lechtman et al. 1982).

FIG. 15

*(top) Solid
metal form
for shaping a
sheet metal
figure.
H. 11.2 cms.*

FIGS. 16A, B

*(bottom)
Sheet metal
owl figure
made over
the form
shown in
Figure 15.
H. 11.4 cms.*

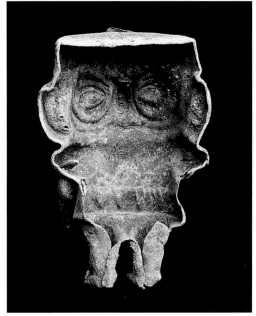

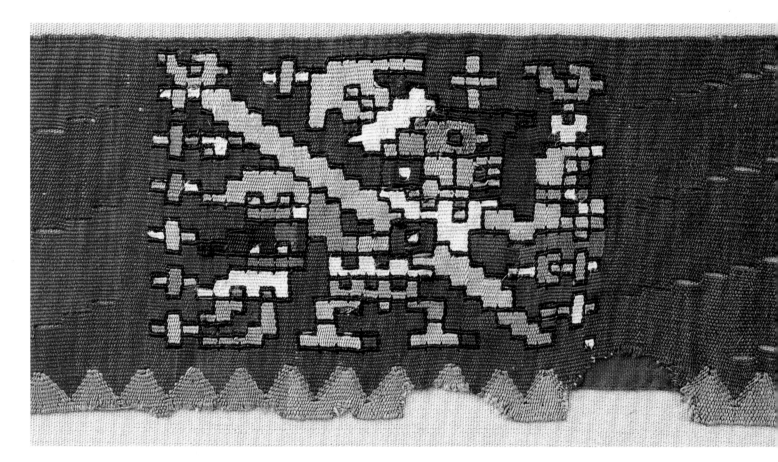

FIG. 17

*Tapestry with
warrior design.
H. of figures
7.3 cms.*

Moche metalworkers also developed a means of gilding copper objects by electrochemical plating. Their procedure was to dissolve gold in a solution of water and corrosive minerals such as ordinary salt and potassium nitrate. To this solution they added a compound such as bicarbonate of soda to achieve a pH of about nine. A clean copper object, dipped into this solution when it was gently boiling, served as both anode and cathode, and a thin coating of gold formed on its surface. Then the object was heated to a temperature between 500° and 800°C (932° to 1472°F) to bond the gold permanently to the copper (*ibid.*).

While Moche ceramics and metal objects are generally well preserved, only a few of their textiles have survived. Nevertheless, they provide ample testimony to the skill of Moche weavers, who created sumptuous fabrics from cotton and wool (Fig. 17). The cotton was grown locally and was normally spun into yarn in a clockwise direction. Wool, on the other hand, was spun in a counterclockwise direction, suggesting that it may have been produced by non-Moche people. It may have been acquired as yarn from llama and alpaca herders living in the Andean highlands.

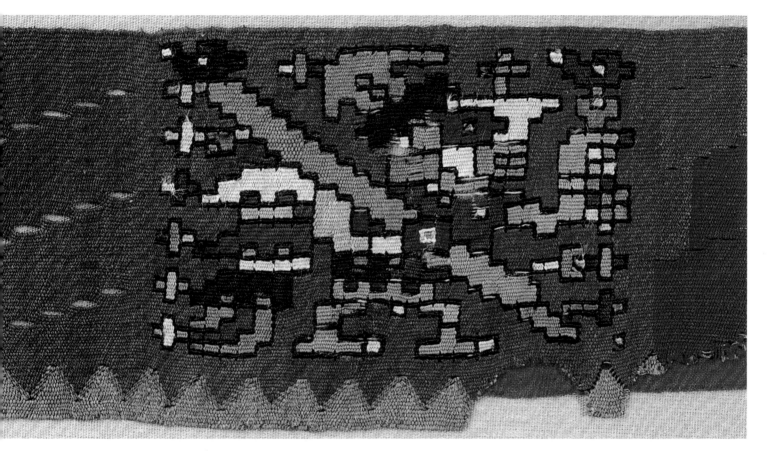

The basic technique for weaving elaborate textiles — using a backstrap loom and multicolored wool yarns to create slit tapestries — was developed in the Andean area centuries before the Moche. However, the Moche were first to innovate the great variety of twill weaves that became a major aspect of their textile industry. They were also the first to cover woven garments with gilded metal platelets, producing clothing that appeared to be made of gold.

In addition to ceramics, metallurgy, and weaving, Moche art was expressed in carved and inlaid bone, wood, and stone, as well as in pyroengraved gourds and colorful wall murals. In all, thousands of examples of Moche art have survived through the centuries to provide present-day researchers with tantalizing views of Moche life. Thus, the Moche left a vivid artistic record of their activities, environment, and supernatural realm.

Moche civilization suddenly collapsed about A.D. 800. The explanation for that mysterious event may lie in the natural cataclysms that periodically devastate coastal Peru. Calamitous earthquakes can uplift and buckle the land, a sporadic weather disruption known as El Niño sometimes unleashes torrential rains, and decade-long droughts have been known to shrivel the harvests. By the time the Spaniards arrived in the early sixteenth century, winds and periodic rains had eroded Moche adobe pyramids and palaces, and in many areas drifting sand dunes had quietly moved in to bury their agricultural fields, canal systems, and villages.

Since the Moche had no writing system, they left no written records to help us understand the nature of their civilization. Moreover, because their civilization ended centuries before European contact, there are no first-hand accounts like those available to help us reconstruct Inca civilization. Instead, nearly everything we know about the Moche has come from archaeological investigation. Fortunately, archaeological research in this area is unusually productive. As in ancient Egypt, organic materials such as plant remains, basketry, leather, and even human bodies are often remarkably well preserved by arid climatic conditions. Consequently, abundant material is available today for archaeologists seeking a detailed reconstruction of ancient Moche society.

The first scientific excavation of Moche material occurred in 1899, when the German archaeologist Max Uhle excavated thirty-one burials at the pyramids near the present-day village of Moche.[2] The name of that village was ultimately used as the name of the ancient civilization.

After Uhle's pioneering work, it was a Peruvian, Rafael Larco Hoyle, who made the greatest contribution to our understanding of Moche civilization. Though not formally trained in archaeology, Larco was the first to attempt a systematic reconstruction of the culture of the Moche. He accomplished this through excavation, painstaking observation of Moche iconography and art, clues provided by early Spanish documents, and analysis of cultural traditions still practiced by the people of northern Peru.[3]

[2] Uhle's excavations were supported by Phoebe Apperson Hearst, whose son William Randolph Hearst became a major newspaper publisher. Uhle's collections went to the museum at the University of California at Berkeley, where they have remained. They are still considered to be among the finest Moche research collections in the world.
[3] Larco developed a remarkable collection of archaeological material, which became the splendid Rafael Larco Herrera Museum in Lima.

Since Larco's work, additional archaeological research has shed more light on various aspects of Moche culture. Most of the valleys on the north coast of Peru have been explored and their archaeological sites systematically recorded. Scores of Moche sites have been identified, and many have been excavated. As a result, we have a fairly good sense of Moche settlement patterns and the nature of various-sized Moche communities, from farmsteads and small villages to large settlements with populations of as many as 10,000 inhabitants.

More than 350 Moche burials have been scientifically excavated, showing a range of elaboration in funerary practice. In the simplest burials the deceased was merely wrapped in a plain cotton shroud and placed in a shallow pit. In more elaborate burials the body was either wrapped in multiple shrouds and twined cane matting, or placed in a box-like cane coffin.

The most elaborate Moche burials typically are found at major Moche settlements with large pyramid structures. Normally, the deceased was placed in a small rectangular chamber with stone or mud-brick walls, roofed with cane or wood beams. The more elaborate the technique of wrapping or encasing the body, the more complex the funerary chamber, and the higher the quantity and quality of grave contents.

Overall, the range of elaboration and complexity of Moche burial practice, as it was known prior to 1987, indicated a highly stratified society. The elite clearly had more access to power and wealth than the common people, but there appeared to have been an unbroken continuum from rich to poor. In 1987, however, astounding new burial material was found which dramatically expanded our understanding of Moche civilization. That year would witness one of the most spectacular archaeological discoveries ever made — the royal tombs at Sipán.

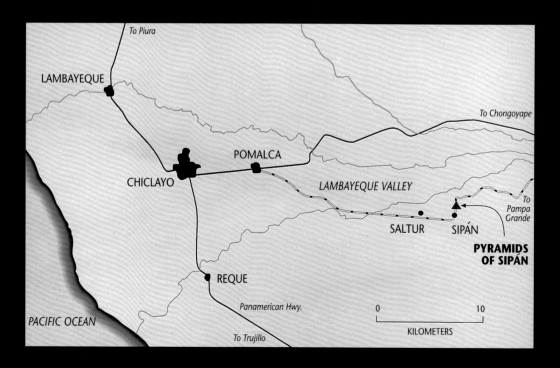

To Piura

LAMBAYEQUE

To Chongoyape

POMALCA

CHICLAYO

LAMBAYEQUE VALLEY

To Pampa Grande

SALTUR   SIPÁN

PYRAMIDS OF SIPÁN

REQUE

Panamerican Hwy.

0   10

KILOMETERS

PACIFIC OCEAN

To Trujillo

FIG. 18
─────
(top)
Map of the
Lambayeque
area.

FIG. 19
─────
(bottom)
Air photo of the
pyramids at Sipán.
The first pyramid,
in the foreground,
is the largest. The
second pyramid
is intermediate
in size, and the
third pyramid
is the smallest.

A ROYAL TOMB IS LOOTED

▼ Sipán is a village of approximately 1,500 people, located in the central part of the Lambayeque River valley (Fig. 18). The combination of abundant water resources and rich, flat farmland has made this area ideal for intensive agricultural production for thousands of years. Today it is planted almost exclusively in sugar cane, although in the past the crops were more diversified.

For decades the ancient pyramids and cemeteries in the vicinity of Sipán have been sporadically looted by the local people who, either individually or in small groups, dig deep holes with picks and shovels in the hope of locating an unlooted tomb. They normally find ceramic vessels, shell or stone beads, or objects of copper that can be sold to the antiquities dealers who intermittently come through the area. But on rare occasions, a tomb is found that contains objects of silver or gold — perhaps a necklace of hollow beads, a nose ornament, or a pair of ear ornaments. The prospect of finding such a tomb, plus the minimal income derived from the more mundane objects that are continually being found, keeps the looters motivated.

Most of the men who loot in this area do so on a part-time basis, during periods when there is no work available in the sugar cane fields and they are in need of supplementary income. Very few do it full-time, or prefer it to other ways of earning money. Yet the tradition of looting that has continued for generations has resulted in a widespread knowledge of looting techniques, the places where one is likely to find intact graves, and even the ways of dealing with local police and governmental authorities who are responsible for the protection of archaeological monuments.

Near the village of Sipán an impressive cluster of pyramids rises dramatically out of the intensively cultivated valley floor (Fig. 19).[4] They are visible from miles away, their heavily eroded surfaces giving them the appearance of natural hills. But they are made of hundreds of thousands of sun-dried mud bricks, mortared into position, creating large solid structures.

By November of 1986, local looters had nearly exhausted the cemeteries in the area of Sipán. One group decided to return to the pyramids to search once again for unlooted tombs. They focused their attention on the smallest of the three pyramids (Fig. 20), and began digging a series of deep holes into its solid matrix of mud bricks. To avoid police detection they worked only at night. After many weeks, they had dug numerous holes, but had found very little of value. They then began a pit near the northwest corner of the pyramid's summit (Fig. 20), once again digging down through the hard matrix until they reached a depth of approximately seven meters. At about ten o'clock on

---

[4] This cluster of pyramids is often referred to as Huaca Rajada, and is generally identified by that term on maps of the archaeological sites of Peru.

FIG. 20

*The smallest pyramid at Sipán
as seen from the summit of the
adjacent pyramid, April 1987.
The arrow indicates the pit where
the royal tomb was looted.*

the night of February 16, 1987, the men digging at the bottom of the pit suddenly broke into one of the richest funerary chambers ever looted — the royal tomb of an ancient Moche ruler.

Accounts vary as to what was found, but most claim that several rice sacks (approximately the size of gunnysacks) of gold, silver, and gilded copper objects were removed. Some ceramic vessels were taken, but many more were broken and left scattered by the looters, who hastily tore through the funerary contents in search of the gold and silver objects.

Almost immediately, arguments broke out over how the treasure was to be divided. Shortly thereafter, one looter, who was displeased with his paltry share of the find, contacted the police and informed on what he and his comrades had done.

The police went to the village of Sipán, where they raided the home of several brothers who had participated in the looting operation. In the process, they seized some of the plundered artifacts and arrested two suspects for questioning. Returning to police headquarters in Chiclayo with the suspects and confiscated material, they telephoned Walter Alva, Director of the Bruning Museum in the nearby town of Lambayeque. For years Alva had worked closely with the police in an effort to combat the looting of archaeological sites, and the police had routinely turned over to the Bruning Museum all Pre-Columbian objects that they confiscated from looters or from the antiquities dealers who trafficked in the looted material. But never before had they confiscated anything remotely as significant as the objects seized in the raid at Sipán — nothing as valuable, nor of such scientific importance.

When Alva arrived at the police headquarters, he was shown the confiscated material. Laid out on a large table were more than thirty objects of Moche metal. Many were nearly pure gold, while others were silver or gilded copper. The exquisite craftsmanship on some of them surpassed anything previously known to have been produced by the Moche. Alva's initial examination of these treasures left him stunned!

It was imperative that the looted tomb be located, and that every effort be made to learn as much as possible about its original form and contents. Almost immediately, Alva and the police returned to the village of Sipán. News of the find had spread rapidly among the local residents and they had been flocking to the pyramids in mass in the hope of finding additional tombs, or objects from the opened tomb that its looters may have missed. Men, women, and even young children had come to the site with collanders or pieces of window screen to sift through the backdirt from the looted tomb. Some found turquoise beads, discs of gilded copper, and in some instances even small gold objects.

The people were reluctant to leave when the police arrived, and it took several hours of persuasive action before they started to move off the pyramid. Eventually they dispersed and returned to their homes, but it was clear that unless the site was guarded day and night, they would quickly return and the pyramid would be destroyed.

Already a great deal of damage had been done by the original grave robbers and by the subsequent crowds of people who had entered the chamber and hacked at its side walls. Using a long cane ladder, it was possible to climb down into the looted funerary chamber (Figs. 21, 22), but it had been so badly damaged that its size and form would be nearly impossible to reconstruct. Where once there had been a tomb of astounding wealth and monumental importance to archaeological research, there was now only an irregular boot-shaped hole.

Walter Alva decided that an archaeological project should be organized immediately to map the pyramid, investigate its construction, and learn everything possible about the context of the looted tomb. The police agreed to post guards at the site around the clock — four officers armed with submachine guns. He proceeded to set up camp and begin. It was thought that the project might last as long as three months, depending largely on what financial support could be obtained from local patrons. There was no time to plan the work in advance or solicit funds from granting agencies, only time to move forward and do whatever was possible to record archaeologically a site that was surely doomed. He knew that as long as the archaeological work continued and the police guard was maintained, the site would be protected. It was in this spirit that the work began.

Meanwhile, the looters were able to hide the bulk of the treasure they had pillaged from the tomb and to slowly sell off items through a diverse network of antiquities dealers and their intermediaries. Necklaces, bracelets, and other ornaments were taken apart and their beads sold piecemeal. As the objects came onto the art market in Lima, Peru's capital city, collectors were dazzled by the exquisite quality of the workmanship. Prices rapidly escalated. Some objects were purchased by Peruvian collectors, while others were illegally exported to be sold in Europe, Japan, and the United States. Within months, the tomb contents were so widely dispersed that there was little hope of reconstructing an inventory of what the looters had found.

It was fortunate that at least some objects from the tomb had been confiscated during the police raid, and ultimately transferred to the permanent collection of the Bruning Museum. In June, 1987, a second group of objects from the looted tomb was confiscated by the police and was also given to the Bruning Museum. Although these two lots constituted a pitifully small fraction of the entire hoard, they provided a tantalizing glimpse of its original splendor.

FIG. 21

(top) The entrance
to the looted tomb
chamber, April 1987.

FIG. 22

(bottom) Looking down
into the looted tomb
chamber, April 1987.

FIG. 23

Gold human-head
bead with silver and
lapis lazuli eyes.
H. 12.5 cms.

The majority of the objects were hollow beads, made in a wondrous variety of shapes and sizes. Each was crafted of two sheets of metal which were soldered together around their edges. One of the largest, and certainly the most spectacular, was a human head of nearly pure gold, 12.5 centimeters high (Fig. 23). The eyes were silver, with pupils of precious lapis lazuli.

Two other large beads were in the form of feline heads (Figs. 24, 25). Each was sixteen centimeters in diameter, with a lenticular cross section. They were made of gilded copper, and had eyes and teeth of inlaid shell.

There were five spherical beads of different sizes ranging between sixteen and twenty-two millimeters in diameter (Fig. 26), and four beads were in the shape of peanuts with long ridges curving along the length of the peanut shell (Fig. 27). Two of the peanuts were gold, and two were silver. The largest was nine centimeters long.

Additional bead shapes included a string of 203 tiny spherical and cylindrical gold beads ranging between two and three millimeters in diameter (Fig. 28), and three types of long trapezoidal gold beads (Figs. 29, 30, 31).

FIG. 24

(left) Gilded copper feline-head bead with shell teeth. H. 16 cms.

FIG. 25

(right) Gilded copper feline-head bead with shell teeth. H. 16 cms.

FIG. 26

(top) Gold
spherical beads.
Dia. of largest
2.2 cms.

FIG. 27

(bottom)
Gold and silver
peanut beads.
Length of largest
9 cms.

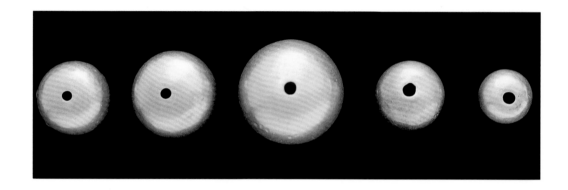

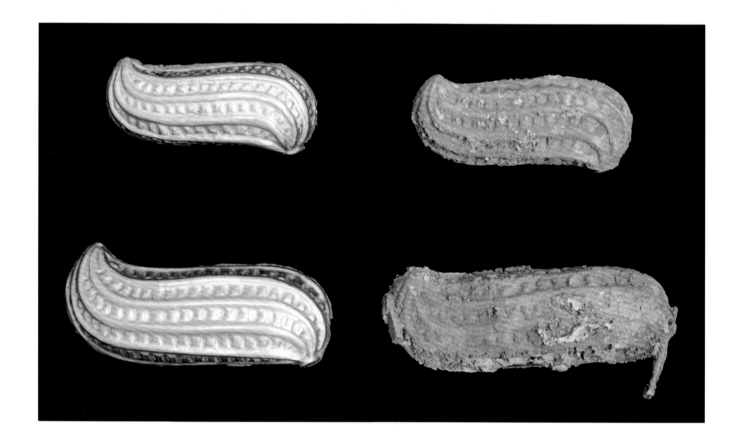

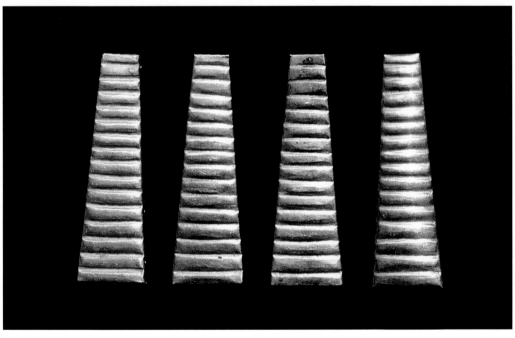

FIG. 28
———
(top) Tiny
gold beads.
Dia. of largest
0.3 cm.

FIG. 29
———
(bottom)
Trapezoidal
gold beads.
H. 8.6 cms.

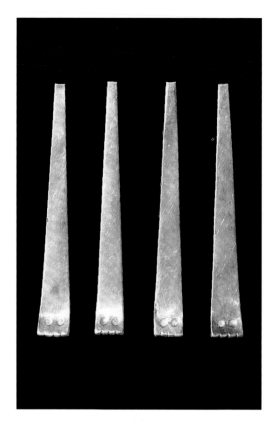

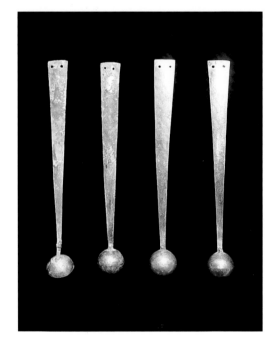

FIG. 30
———
(top)
Trapezoidal
gold beads.
H. 20.5 cms.

FIG. 31
———
(bottom)
Trapezoidal
gold beads
with spheres.
H. 11.5 cms.

As we carefully examined this marvelous array of beads, we wondered how they might have been strung. If only they had not been torn from their original context! Were beads of different types originally strung together on a single necklace? Were necklaces made up of beads of a single metal, or could silver beads be strung with gold or gilded copper beads? We tried endless combinations, putting them in what seemed like every conceivable juxtaposition, but in the end we were unable to determine how they had been assembled. Perhaps we would never know.

In addition to the beads, there were two ear ornaments of a type frequently worn by high status Moche males. They consisted of large circular front pieces, mounted on tubular posts projecting backwards. The posts were inserted through an enlarged perforation in each ear lobe, and thus hung back along the sides of the wearer's neck while the ornamental front pieces flanked the wearer's face, as can be seen in the ceramic portrait in Figure 32.

The looted ear ornaments, one of gold and the other of silver, were ten centimeters in diameter (Fig. 33). Tiny spheres were edge-welded around the periphery of each ear ornament. Small circular platelets hung from wires covering the front sides. When the ear ornaments were worn, these bangles would have been in constant motion, shimmering with reflected light. We wondered if the gold and silver ear orna-

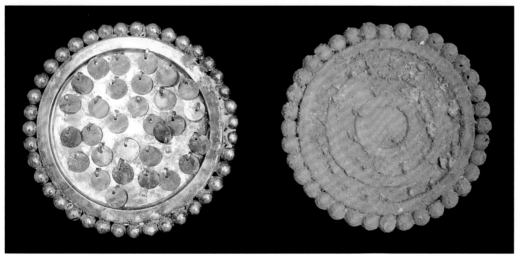

FIG. 32
——
(top) Bowl
depicting a
man wearing
large ear
ornaments.
Not found
at Sipán.

FIG. 33
——
(bottom)
A gold and
a silver ear
ornament.
Dia. 10 cms.

FIG. 34

Jar depicting a
man wearing
a variety of
ornaments.
Not found
at Sipán.
H. 32 cms.

ments were originally a pair, meant to be worn together — or were there originally two pairs, one of gold and one of silver?

Another item among the material seized by the police was a spectacular semi-circular bell (Fig. 35). Similar bells are sometimes seen in Moche art, hanging from the belts of warriors (Fig. 34). This example was made from a circular sheet of gilded copper, with sixteen half-spheres hammered around its periphery. Within the circle of half-spheres were two deity figures that were mirror images of one another, connected across the tops of their headdresses. The circular sheet was then folded along this connection, so the object became a semi-circle. A pellet of copper was placed inside each of the spheres along the periphery, creating an eight-chambered bell. Hung from a warrior's belt, these bells would have jingled at the slightest movement.

FIG. 35

Gilded copper bell. H. 12 cms.

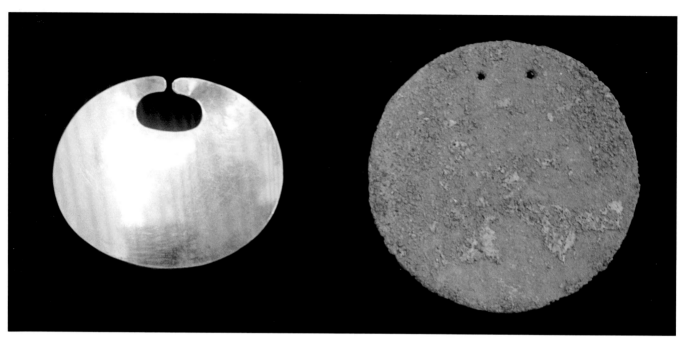

FIG. 36

Gold nose
ornament
H. 3.2 cms.
and silver disc
Dia. 4.5 cms.

Yet another item was a gold nose ornament (Fig. 36, left). It was oval and slightly concave, with a beautifully polished surface, and must once have adorned the nose of an elite male. High status Moche males had their noses perforated through the septum in order to wear nose jewelry.

The seized material also included several items whose purpose was enigmatic. Among these were a silver disc, 4.5 centimeters in diameter, with two holes near its outer edge (Fig. 36, right); a gold disc, four centimeters in diameter, with a circle and checkerboard pattern very lightly incised in its polished surface (Fig. 37, left); a spherical bell, 2.5 centimeters in diameter, made of a single sheet of gold, with scroll designs incised on its outer surface (Fig. 37, center); and a gilded copper cone (Fig. 37, right), 3.5 centimeters high, with horizontal bands embossed on its surface.

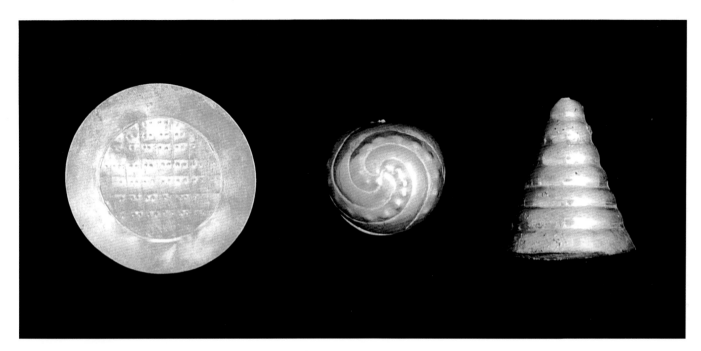

FIG. 37

Gold disc
Dia. 4 cms.,
gold spherical bell
Dia. 2.5 cms.,
and gilded
copper cone
H. 3.5 cms.

Certainly these objects must originally have been pieces of something else. But what? There was nothing like them in museums or private collections, and we were unable to relate them directly to any objects seen in Moche art. We could only speculate about their original function.

Little did we realize that as our excavation proceeded at Sipán we would find the answers to our questions. Ultimately, these objects, which seemed so strange and puzzling out of context, were to become known and familiar to us. Moreover, they were to provide valuable information not only about the Moche people, but also about the specific individual whose royal tomb had been so ruthlessly torn apart by the looters. The answers to all our questions, and more, would be revealed by the archaeological work that was underway at Sipán.

FIG. 38

(top) Sipán in 1988 with the excavation underway at the small pyramid in the lower left. View is toward the southwest.

FIG. 39

(bottom) Sipán as it may have appeared seventeen hundred years ago. View is toward the southwest.

▼ The pyramids near Sipán were virtually unknown before our work began. Since they had never been scientifically excavated or even mapped, our first objectives would be to define the overall size and form of the monumental construction, and determine when the pyramid complex was built. We began by making a contour map of the three pyramids and what remained of their ramps and adjacent plazas (Fig. 38). This ultimately made it possible to reconstruct how the site may have appeared in ancient times (Fig. 39).

The two large truncated pyramids were connected by a complex series of ramps, and had a large rectangular platform extending toward the north. The smaller truncated pyramid, where the tomb had been looted, appears to have been free-standing, connected to the larger pyramids only by a large plaza. It had a long platform on its north side and a shorter platform on its south side. A ramp on the north platform gave access to the summit, on which stood a small solid structure.

It became clear that the enormous architectural complex at Sipán was constructed over a period of many years and had experienced numerous changes as the various parts were enlarged. We found some evidence that the two large pyramids were further modified after the Moche occupation, but the bulk of their structure appears to have been built by the Moche. It may be, however, that deep inside one or more of these pyramids, or well beneath their surrounding patios, there is even architecture preceding that of the Moche.

While the overall complex of pyramids at Sipán was being mapped, special attention was given to the small pyramid where the looted tomb had been found. It was much more heavily damaged than the two larger pyramids. For generations, grave robbers had relentlessly mined the structure in search of tombs. Their holes penetrated far into its bulk, producing a complex maze of interconnected tunnels that branched out like roots of a tree from deep central shafts. The holes had destroyed parts of the original pyramid, and huge piles of backdirt from the illicit tunneling had been dumped outside the mouths of the shafts or over the side of the structure, so that much of its original form was no longer visible.

In some instances, however, the looters' backdirt had actually served to protect the structure's original form, a form that could be revealed when the backdirt was carefully removed. Moreover, by cleaning out the maze of holes that had been dug into the pyramid, we were able to climb down inside it and study the construction of its massive bulk. Subtle features of its internal architecture clearly indicated that it had undergone successive periods of construction.

One member of the Sipán archaeological team, Susana Meneses, systematically began to compile and analyze all of the information that could be obtained regarding the construction sequence. She

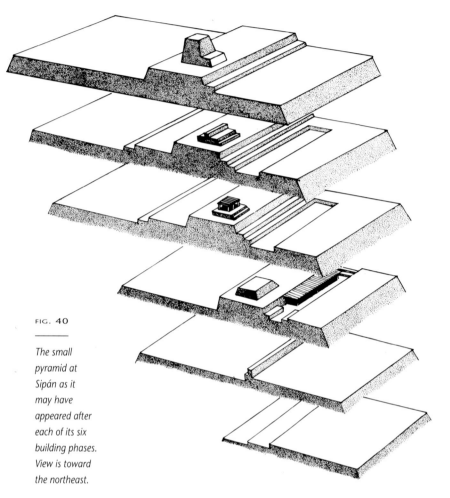

FIG. 40
———
The small
pyramid at
Sipán as it
may have
appeared after
each of its six
building phases.
View is toward
the northeast.

combined what was revealed by the looters' pits with what could be learned from the ongoing archaeological excavation. Of particular interest were subtle differences in the size, form, color, and composition of the mud bricks, the mortar used in setting them, and the plaster used on walls and floors. These differences were clues to various phases of construction. Ultimately, the diligence and painstaking attention to detail by Susana Meneses paid off — she was able to demonstrate that the structure had evolved through at least six building phases, with each new construction encapsulating the previous ones (Fig. 40).

In its earliest phase, the pyramid appears to have been a low, rectangular platform with two steps extending along the full length of its north side. It was subsequently enlarged toward the north, and a transverse wall was built that spanned the summit east-west. The third phase saw the addition of a covered corridor, the func-

tion of which we can only guess. Over the next three construction phases, the structure continued to grow toward the north and to acquire greater height. This ultimately resulted in a truncated pyramid near the central section, with low platforms extending north and south.

Although we do not know with certainty when the first construction was completed, we suspect that it may have been during the first century A.D. The sixth construction phase must have been completed by A.D. 300.

While the looters' pits were being cleared and systematically studied, we paid particular attention to the pit that had recently reached the plundered tomb. We began immediately to map it and to draw profiles of its form. We also sifted through the loose soil and debris inside it and around its

FIG. 41

Gilded
copper
crown.
H. 16 cms.

opening in an effort to locate objects that could provide further information about its contents. Unfortunately, little remained of the tomb's original form or contents. The local people who came after the looters had not only hacked ruthlessly at the sides of the chamber, but dug short, irregular tunnels radiating out from it like spokes on a wheel. Moreover, they had sifted and resifted the looters' backdirt, removing nearly everything that had been left from the original plunder.

Nevertheless, by carefully studying the upper part of the burial chamber we were able to determine that it was roofed with large wood beams. These beams, which had decomposed to a light grey powder, were laid horizontally and parallel to one another. They were oriented east-west, suggesting that if the burial chamber had been rectangular, it was probably oriented with its length north-south and its width east-west.

To our great surprise, we were also able to uncover some of the original tomb contents that had been missed by both the original looters and the local people who followed them. Clearing along one side of the burial chamber, we found the remains of a large object of gilded copper (Fig. 41). It was

FIG. 42
─────
(top)
Ceramic jars.
H. of tallest
21.5 cms.

FIG. 43
─────
(bottom)
Copper
mask with
turquoise eyes.
H. 20.5 cms.

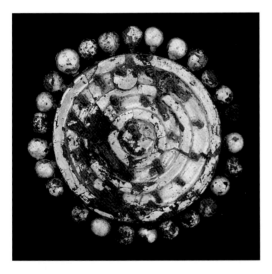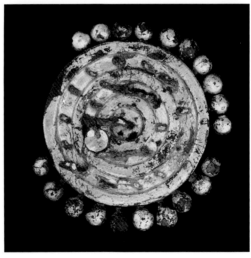

FIG. 44

(top) Gilded copper
owl-head bead.
H. 4 cms.

FIGS. 45, 46

(bottom)
Gilded copper
ear ornaments.
Dia. 6.5 cms.

badly broken, and parts of it were missing, but it appeared to have been a tall crown, ornamented with metal discs suspended from wires. We also found four complete ceramic jars with chambers modeled in the form of human figures (Fig. 42). We carefully removed the soil around these objects, ultimately freeing them from the matrix in which they had been embedded for centuries. In the process, we discovered the edge of a life-sized copper mask with inlaid turquoise eyes (Fig. 43).

Near the copper mask were two owl-head beads of gilded copper, each four centimeters high (Fig. 44), and a pair of gilded copper ear ornaments, 6.5 centimeters in diameter (Figs. 45, 46). The latter resembled the larger gold and silver ear ornaments confiscated by the police (Fig. 33), but only a few of the small dangling circular platelets were still attached.

As these objects were excavated, we uncovered something even more remarkable — a heavy

FIG. 47

Walter Alva
inside the
looted tomb
chamber,
holding the
copper scepter.
H. of scepter
100 cms.

FIG. 48

*Top of the
copper scepter.
W. 16.5 cms.*

copper scepter, one meter long, with a point at one end and a complex architectural model at the other (Figs. 47, 48). The architecture consisted of a small central structure with a gabled roof sitting on a square platform. A double row of mace heads formed a balustrade around the four sides of the central structure. On the ridgeline of the roof were seventeen double-faced human heads. The structure was open on its front and sides, but the back was formed by a wall bearing a depiction of a supernatural creature, half feline and half reptile, copulating with a woman on a crescent moon.

This scepter must have been a prized piece of ceremonial paraphernalia, the property of someone of exceedingly high status in Moche society. It was clearly commensurate with the power of the Moche lord whose spectacularly rich tomb had been recently plundered.

Could it be that the structure with the gabled roof was his palace or temple? Might it have been the one constructed at the summit of this pyramid, or nearby? These and many more questions were on our minds as we completed our study of the looted burial chamber and began to turn our attention to what remained of the pyramid's summit.

When we first began our excavation at Sipán, we discussed the possibility of opening a large excavation unit at the summit. We knew that as soon as our investigation ended and the site was left unguarded, looters would return and completely destroy the pyramid in a period of months. At least if we excavated the core, it could provide valuable information about the site, and this information would be available to scholars in future years.

FIG. 49

*Ceramic vessels
in Offering 1.*

We surveyed the entire pyramid, and then chose a ten by ten meter area near its summit. This was then divided into four squares, five meters on each side, and each of these was further divided into units of one square meter. After recording all surface features, we began excavating selected squares. In most of our excavation area, we found a hard matrix of mud bricks that had been mortared in place with clay as the pyramid was constructed. The excavation was a slow and difficult process, for each layer had to be cleaned, drawn, and the loose bricks removed individually.

Near the northwest corner of our excavation there was a place where centuries ago the bricks had apparently been removed and subsequently replaced with loosely compacted sand and small stones. As we began removing this material we found eight decomposed wood beams, similar to those that had roofed the looted burial chamber. They were horizontal, parallel to one another, and had roofed a small rectangular chamber about 2.90 meters long, 1.80 meters wide, and 1.25 meters deep. We recorded and then removed the powdered residue of the roof and began excavating below it. Suddenly we came upon the lid of a red clay pot, and our excitement grew. Then many more ceramics were uncovered — bowls, jars, and bottles. We eventually removed 1,137 vessels from the chamber, perhaps the largest offering of Pre-Columbian ceramics ever excavated (Figs. 49, 50).

FIG. 50

Cleaning the ceramics from Offering 1.

FIG. 51

Examples of the
ceramics from
Offering 1.
H. of tallest
21.8 cms.

The majority of the ceramics were jars (Fig. 51) similar to the ones we had found in the looted tomb. They depicted a variety of human figures: warriors holding warclubs and shields, nude prisoners with leash-like ropes around their necks, musicians with drums, seated figures wearing large beaded pectorals, and jars with schematic human features. The coarse surfaces on these pots, their absence of wear, and their often identical shapes suggested that they had been mass-produced in molds shortly before being placed in the chamber. Some appeared to have been deliberately arranged in symbolic tableaux, like figures of a Christmas crèche. Musicians and prisoners, for example, ringed and faced nobler personages. Some trooped double file, while others appeared to be alone and apart, or placed adjacent to clusters of llama bones or sea shells. Also found among the ceramic vessels were pieces of copper, including a naturalistic human mask and several copper sheets that were probably parts of elaborate headdresses.

A macabre final discovery awaited us in this pottery-filled chamber. A man's skeleton lay jack-knifed on its back, with chin, knees, and arms pulled in toward the torso. Since the Moche buried their dead in a fully extended position, lying on their backs with their arms at their sides, it seemed likely that this individual was a sacrificial victim, whose body had been shoved into the small chamber as part of the ritual offering. We gave the chamber the designation "Offering 1," with the optimistic hope that we might locate others. Little did we know at that time that we were soon to find something even more wonderful nearby. We were about to discover the undisturbed royal tomb of an ancient Moche lord.

FIG. 52

Excavation at the
summit of the small
pyramid at Sipán.
Offering 1 is in the
lower left, and the
second area of fill
is beneath the
horizontal ladder.

IV T HE EXCAVATION OF TOMB 1

▼ As Offering 1 was being excavated, we discovered another area of fill about three meters to the southeast (Fig. 52). It contained the same kind of soil found in the upper part of Offering 1, and it was clearly another place where bricks had been removed from the pyramid, and the area subsequently filled. Would it contain another offering? Or an ancient tomb?

We began removing the fill, and, to our amazement, found that it defined a rectangular area approximately five meters on each side. If it proved to be as deep as it was wide, it would be a large, room-sized chamber.

Over a period of weeks we slowly excavated the fill to a depth of about four meters below the original surface of the pyramid. There we found the skeleton of a man wrapped in a cotton shroud. He lay on his back in an extended position, with his right forearm over his chest. In his left hand and mouth were lumps of copper. He wore a gilded copper helmet, and resting on his right forearm was a round copper shield. Perhaps in life he had been a warrior, similar to those frequently depicted in Moche art. Analysis of his skeleton indicated that he had died at about twenty years of age. Although he exhibited no signs of violent death, his feet were missing. It was not possible to determine if they had been amputated during his life or after his death.

Approximately fifty centimeters beneath the burial of this man, we found the remains of large wood beams. They had decomposed long ago to a grey powder, but the impressions they left in the soil allowed us to reconstruct their original size and form. Seventeen parallel beams had extended across the room from east to west. They had been roughhewn and irregular, and some measured as much as twenty centimeters in diameter and four meters in length. These beams were originally supported by two others, positioned along the east and west sides of the room.

Since similar traces of roof beams had been found in the looted burial chamber, our hopes were high that a major tomb might be found below. One thing was certain: the pattern of roof beams was intact. Whatever lay below had remained undisturbed since the original builders set the last beam in place.

FIG. 53

(top) Copper straps used to lash together wood planks.

FIG. 54

(bottom) Clusters of copper straps first appearing at the corners and sides of the coffin.

Almost immediately beneath the beams, we found eight clusters of copper straps that had corroded to a bright green color (Fig. 53). These clusters defined a rectangle on the floor of our excavation, with one cluster at each corner and one midway along each of the four sides (Fig. 54). Nothing like this had ever been found by archaeologists, and at first it was enigmatic. Then we realized that the straps had been used to lash together wood planks to create a large rectangular box. The wood had long since decomposed, leaving a residue similar to that of the roof beams above. Careful excavation revealed that three planks had formed the top of the box, and one plank formed each of its sides. Could this be a royal coffin? It was positioned precisely in the center of the room, and since it was 2.20 meters long and 1.25 meters wide, it could easily accommodate a fully extended adult body.

The most elaborate Moche coffins previously excavated were made of cane, lashed together with sedge ropes. Moreover, in Moche culture metal was not common, and only people of high status had much of it at their disposal. Using metal as a rope substitute to lash planks together implied that this large wooden box belonged to someone of exceedingly high status. If it was indeed a coffin, we reasoned, it could contain the richest Moche burial ever excavated archaeologically. What we never imagined at that time was that it would contain the richest burial ever excavated anywhere in the Western Hemisphere, and would be one of the most significant archaeological discoveries of our generation.

We carefully recorded and then removed the residue of the three planks forming the lid of the box, and came upon a layer of reddish organic material. This, we later realized, was the decomposed remains of a red textile that had served as an outer burial shroud. Under this was another textile shroud covered with circular platelets of gilded copper, each sewn in place. Beneath that textile was yet a third one, covered with square gilded copper platelets. These three large textiles had been wrapped completely around the corpse and grave goods.

As the upper parts of the shrouds were removed, we began to excavate deeper into the coffin, carefully removing the soil that had sifted in over the centuries as the lid slowly decomposed (Fig. 55). In doing so, we exposed a mass of burial goods, including three long lance points (Fig. 56), feathered headdress ornaments, and the remains of a headdress with an elaborate chin strap. In Moche art, such headdresses are generally worn by high status adult males (Fig. 35). On top of the headdress there was a large gold ingot, approximately five centimeters in diameter and one centimeter thick (Figs. 56, 59). The gold was so pure that its surface remained uncorroded. Gleaming brilliantly in the sunlight, it appeared precisely as it had been formed when the molten gold puddled in

FIG. 55

---

*Excavating
inside the
coffin.*

FIG. 56

Upper level
of burial
goods inside
the coffin.

OVERLEAF:

FIG. 57

Exploded
view of the
contents
of the coffin.

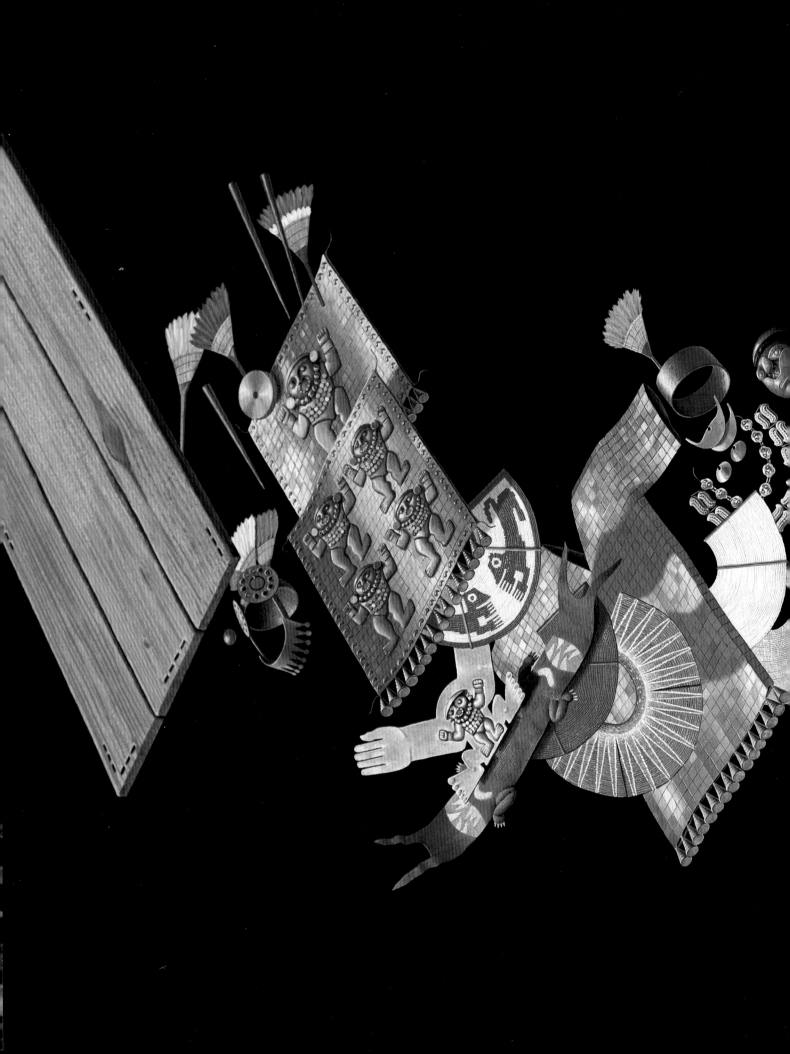

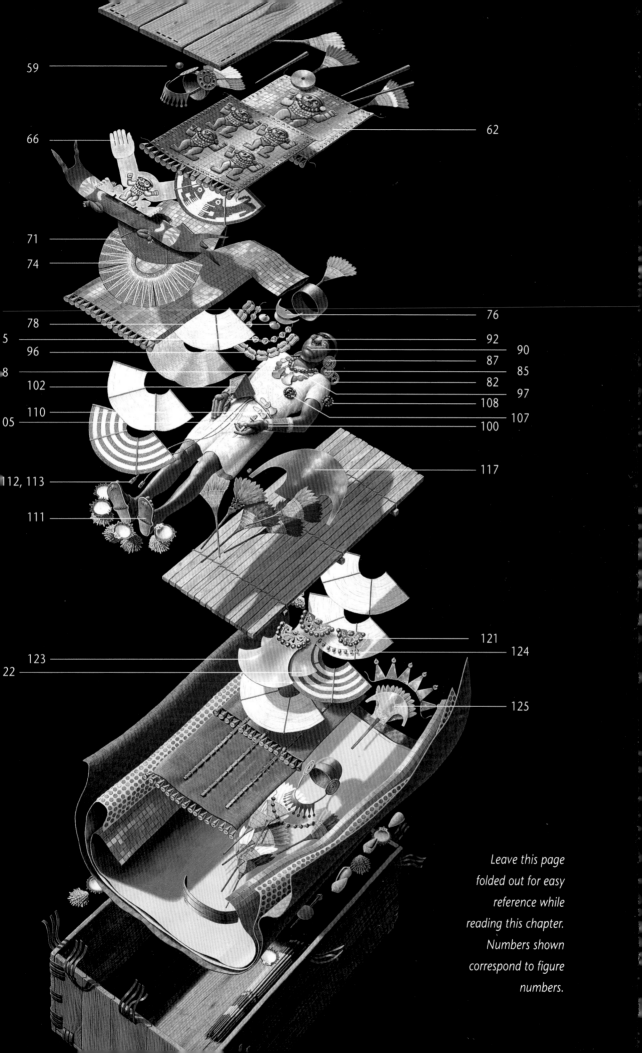

59

62

66

71

74

76

78

5

96

92

90

87

85

8

82

102

97

108

110

107

05

100

112, 113

117

111

121

123

124

22

125

*Leave this page
folded out for easy
reference while
reading this chapter.
Numbers shown
correspond to figure
numbers.*

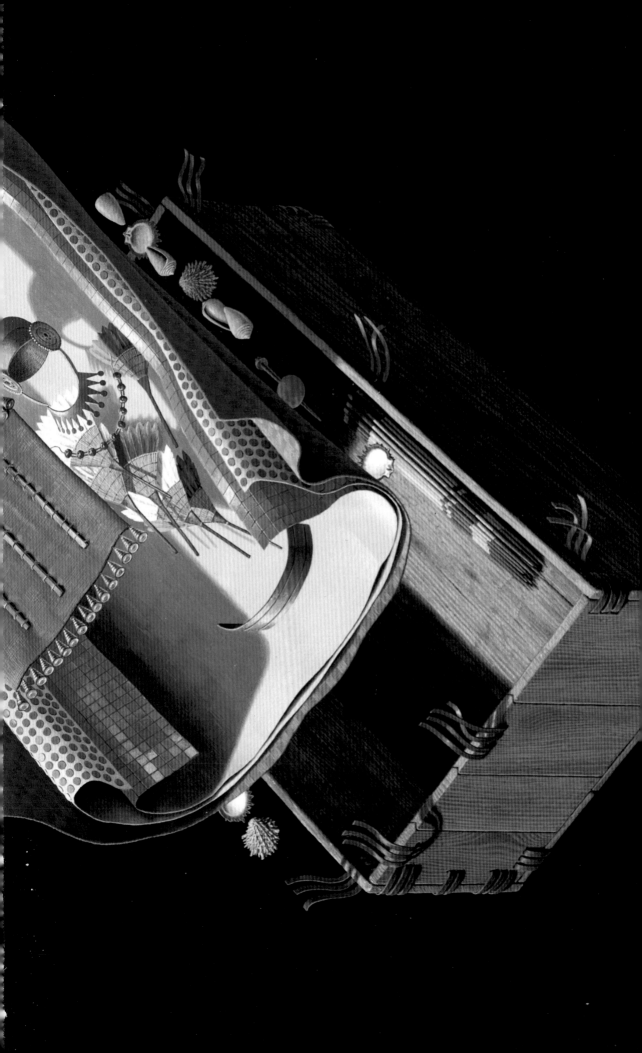

FIG. 58

The individual
lying extended
with head at
the top of the
photo and feet
at the bottom.
A banner is
over the chest.

the bottom of a crucible many centuries ago.

When each of these objects had been recorded and removed, we found the remains of banners, each consisting of two layers of coarse cotton cloth that had been sewn together. Human male figures of sheet metal were sewn to the upper surface of each banner (Fig. 58): apparently four figures on one, and one on the other. The figures were nearly identical. Each was frontal, with the arms raised and the feet pointed out to the sides (Fig. 60). Suspended by wires from the torso of each figure were small sheet metal discs, and triangles hung from the waist. The wrists were adorned with bracelets of tiny turquoise beads (Fig. 61). Surrounding the figures were square platelets of sheet metal, carefully positioned so they completely covered the remaining surface of the banners. The platelets along the outer edges of the banners were each embossed with a paisley-shaped element called an *ulluchu*. To our surprise, along the lower edge of each banner was a row of metal cones, almost identical in size and form to the metal cone confiscated from the looters (Fig. 37). Finding them in this tomb immediately resolved the question of their function — they clearly served as a decorative fringe and were attached to the lower edge of banners.

FIG. 59

(top left)
Large
gold ingot
Dia. 5 cms.
resting on a
decomposed
headdress.

FIG. 60

(top right)
Detail of the
banner over
the individual's
chest.

FIG. 61

(bottom)
Detail of the
left wrist of the
banner figure,
showing the
bracelet of tiny
turquoise beads.

FIG. 62
———
*The banner
cleaned and
reconstructed.
H. 48.5 cms.*

FIG. 63

*Moche depiction
of two individuals
holding banners.*

Although the sheet metal covering the banners had corroded to a dark green color and appeared to be copper, careful cleaning revealed that it was gilded, and would have appeared to be gold when placed in the grave (Fig. 62).

The function of the banners was not clear. No banners had ever been excavated before, but they are sometimes depicted in Moche art being held by high status males (Fig. 63). Perhaps they served some heraldic purpose.

Beneath the banners we found a large sheet of gilded copper, cut out in the form of a headless figure with long arms and short legs (Figs. 64, 66). At its center, in high relief, was a smaller male figure, almost identical to those on the banners (Fig. 65). Nothing like this object had either been excavated or identified in Moche art, and its function is unknown. It may have been part of a banner or headdress, although it lacked any holes that would have facilitated its attachment to something else.

Beneath the headless figure were small remnants of a broad textile band with a woven teeth-like appliqué at each end. Projecting from the sides of the band were four three-dimensional textile legs and feet with metal claws. We assumed that this textile band was part of a headdress.

FIG. 64

A headless
figure of
gilded copper
over the
individual's
waist.

FIG. 65
———
(top left)
Detail of
individual at
the center of
the headless
figure.

FIG. 66
———
(top right) The
headless figure
cleaned and
reconstructed.
H. 42.5 cms.

FIG. 67
———
(left) Design
incised below
the neck of the
headless figure.

FIG. 68

*Ceramic bottle
showing a seated
figure wearing a
beaded pectoral.
H. 18.3 cms.
Not found at Sipán.*

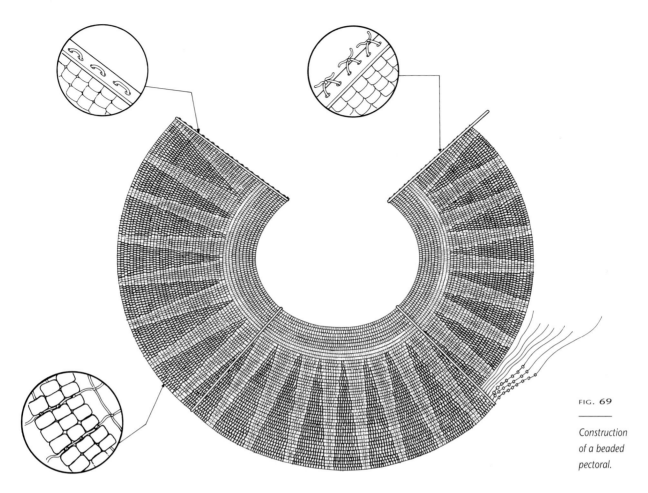

FIG. 69

Construction
of a beaded
pectoral.

At this stage in the excavation, much of the area inside the coffin was covered with beaded pectorals. These are large bib-like objects that are often shown in Moche art being worn by high status males. They cover the chest, extend up over the shoulders, and are tied at the wearer's back (Fig. 68).

Because no complete beaded pectorals had ever been excavated archaeologically, these provided an opportunity to understand their original construction (Fig. 69). Their multiple strands of shell beads were kept parallel to one another by the use of spacer bars — long narrow bands of copper with a series of tiny perforations along their lengths. One spacer bar was at each end of the pectoral, and two others were evenly spaced along its length. The strings on which the beads were strung passed through perforations in the spacer bars, and thus were kept in position in close, parallel rows. The parallel rows were further maintained by being sewn together with rows of fine thread.

Excavating and removing the beaded pectorals presented a formidable challenge (Fig. 70). The tightly spun cotton string that was originally used to assemble them had decomposed to the consistency of ash. Touching it, even with the finest camel-hair brush, caused it to crumble to dust. Although the thousands of beads composing the pectoral lay in their original position, there was

FIG. 70

*A pectoral
of pink shell
beads was
placed over the
individual's
torso.*

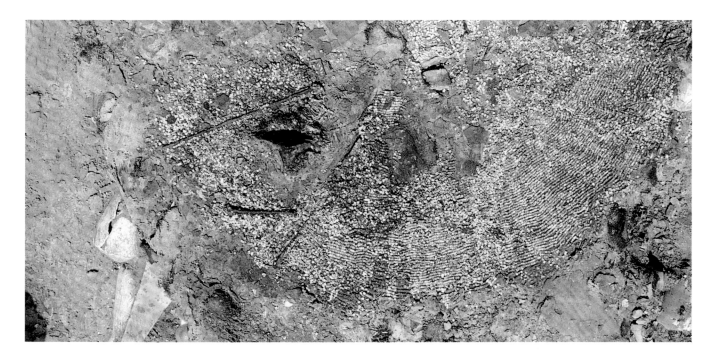

FIG. 71

*Detail of
the pectoral
of pink shell
beads.*

nothing holding them together (Fig. 71). How could they be removed so their position would be maintained, making it possible to reconstruct them later? The difficulty was greatly compounded by the fact that several pectorals had been placed one on top of the other, with nothing separating them. Thus, immediately beneath one layer of beads was another layer belonging to the pectoral below, and beneath those were the beads of yet another pectoral. If beads from different layers became mixed, reconstructing the pectorals accurately would be impossible.

Ultimately, we devised a solution that worked quite well. Using fine brushes and air squeeze bulbs, we painstakingly cleaned the upper surface of one pectoral, making every effort not to move the beads out of position. The beaded design was then photographed and sketched. Next, a thin layer of clean cotton batting was moistened with soluble resin, and carefully patted down on top of the cleaned surface of beads. The soluble resin in the cotton batting stuck to the upper surface of the beads as it dried. We then gently peeled back the cotton, lifting with it an entire sheet of beads. Each bead was held in position adjacent to the beads around it, just as originally strung. The sheets of cotton batting and beads were placed in specially prepared wood trays.

When all the beads and spacer bars of one beaded pectoral were removed, the delicate process began again — patiently cleaning the upper surface of the next pectoral in preparation for its removal with cotton batting. The removal of three pectorals took several weeks, but the results fully justified our care and patience. One of the pectorals was made of white and red shell beads arranged to depict two animal figures; another consisted entirely of pink shell beads. The third bore an

FIG. 72

Pectoral of white, pink, and green shell beads was placed over the individual's torso.

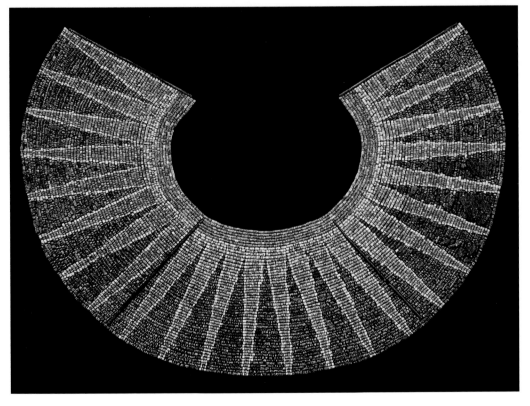

FIG. 73
_____

(top) Detail of
the pectoral of
white, pink, and
green shell beads.

FIG. 74
_____

(bottom)
Pectoral
shown in
Figures 72, 73
cleaned and
reconstructed.
W. 60 cms.

FIG. 75
———
Gold nose
ornaments
in situ.

intricate arrangement of long triangles of white, pink, and green beads (Figs. 72, 73, 74) forming a radiant pattern.[5]

When the three beaded pectorals had been removed, we found beneath them a shirtlike garment. It was covered with square platelets of gilded copper, and, like the banners, may have had gilded copper cones sewn along its hem. It would have been dazzling when worn, with the platelets and cones shimmering and swaying like golden mirrors.

Four more beaded pectorals, very similar in size and form to those above, were found beneath the gilded garment. Again, there was considerable delay as the pectorals were cleaned *in situ* and then painstakingly removed with cotton batting and soluble resin. Two of the pectorals were made exclusively of white shell beads. The third was of yellow shell, and the fourth had horizontal bands of white and red shell beads.

When these four pectorals were removed, it was clear that we were getting close to the body of

[5] The green beads appeared to be copper that had oxidized to a dark green color. When they were analyzed, however, it became clear that they were made of a shell that had absorbed green copper oxide from the corroding copper objects in the tomb. The original color of these shell beads could not be determined.

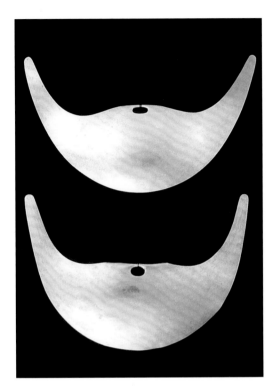

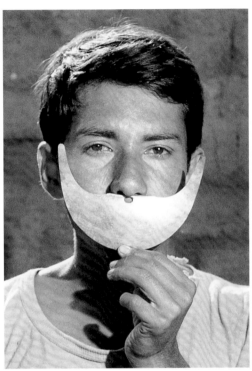

FIG. 76

(left) Pair of gold nose ornaments. H. 10.2 cms. each.

FIG. 77

(right) A gold nose ornament held by one of the students assisting the Sipán excavation.

the person occupying this extraordinary coffin. Bone fragments appeared and began to define the legs and feet, as well as portions of the arms and right wrist. The body was on its back, fully extended, with its arms at its sides and its hands resting above its upper thighs.

As we came closer to the body, the quantity and quality of personal ornaments dramatically increased. Near the face were four metal nose ornaments. Two were large crescents of sheet gold (Figs. 75, 76). Similar nose ornaments are sometimes seen being worn by individuals in Moche art (Fig. 35). In this instance, the crescents were so large that they would have covered the wearer's mouth and most of his lower face (Fig. 77). The other nose ornaments, one gold and one silver, were smaller. Both were oval-shaped and markedly convex (Fig. 78). The gold one was strikingly similar to the gold nose ornament from the looted tomb (Fig. 36).

At the sides of the head were three pairs of exquisite ear ornaments, one depicting deer, another ducks, and the other, warriors (Figs. 79, 80). They combine extraordinary metallurgical and lapidary skill with remarkable artistry, resulting in objects of perfect form, scale, and proportion.

The deer ear ornaments were made by incising the profile of a deer on a disc of sheet gold. The

FIG. 78

———

(top) A gold and a silver nose ornament. H. 7.2 cms. each.

FIG. 79

———

(bottom) Nose ornaments and ear ornaments clustered around the bones of the individual's skull.

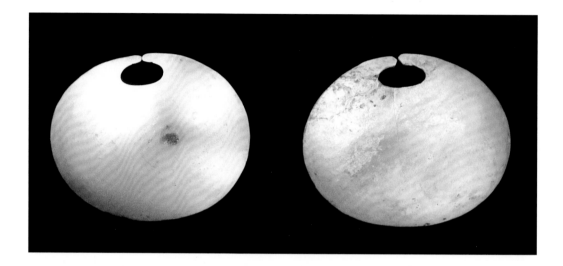

FIG. 80

Ear ornaments
in situ.

FIG. 81

_One of the
deer ear
ornaments
in situ._

background was then cut away so that the deer remained suspended in the center of a sheet metal ring, connected only at the antlers, tongue, hooves, and tail. With the background cut away, the deer appears to be bounding in mid-air (Figs. 81, 82).

The deer and the surrounding ring were covered with a mosaic of gold, white shell, and turquoise. A separate gold ring was fitted over the outer edge of the ear ornament. Around its periphery, tiny hollow spheres of gold had been edge-welded.

The artist who created these extraordinary ear ornaments even finished them on the back side. The gold sheet backing each deer was carefully incised to indicate the animal's eyes, mouth, cloven hooves, and genitals (Fig. 83). The back side would not have been visible when the ear ornaments were being worn. However, anyone examining them by hand, and certainly the person preparing to put them on, would have appreciated this extra detail.

FIG. 82
―――――
(top) The deer
ear ornaments
cleaned and
reconstructed.
Dia. 8.4 cms.
each.

FIG. 83
―――――
(bottom)
Back side of
a deer ear
ornament.

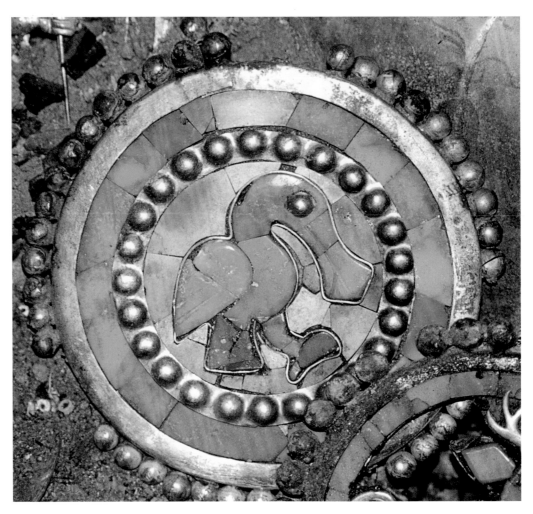

FIG. 84

One of the
duck ear
ornaments
in situ.

FIG. 85

The duck ear
ornaments
cleaned and
reconstructed.
Dia. 9.2 cms.
each.

The duck ear ornaments were equally impressive. They were made of wood discs with gold and turquoise forming a complex mosaic that covered the front side. An evenly wrought gold wire formed the continuous outline of the duck (Fig. 84). Finely faceted pieces of blue-green stone had been cemented inside this wire outline to create the duck, complete with incised lines indicating individual wing feathers. The eye was a tiny half-sphere of gold.

The contrasting lighter green stone mosaics surrounding the duck enhance the beauty of this object. Around the central image is a ring of sheet gold embossed with half-spheres, surrounded by a blue-green stone mosaic. The outer edge is surrounded by a separate gold ring, like that on the deer ear ornaments, with hollow gold spheres edge-welded around its periphery (Fig. 85).

By far the most amazing of the ear ornaments was the pair depicting warriors. The first of these was discovered quite by surprise one afternoon when, in the process of removing the soil near the skull, one of the archaeologists lifted a small dirt clod. His gasp caused all present to turn their attention to this part of the grave. There, after seventeen centuries, was a little warrior of hammered sheet gold, clad in a turquoise tunic (Figs. 86, 87).

Meticulously detailed, the warrior stood about the size of one's thumb, boldly holding a warclub in his clenched fist. A slight twist allowed the warclub to slide free. Made of sheet gold, this club was

FIG. 86

One of the
warrior ear
ornaments
in situ.

FIG. 87

*A warrior ear
ornament
cleaned and
reconstructed.
Dia. 9.4 cms.*

FIG. 88

A warrior ear
ornament
cleaned and
partially
reconstructed.

THE EXCAVATION OF TOMB 1 ▼

a perfect miniature of the ancient military weapon, from the pointed lower end to the tiny club head at the upper end of its long tapering shaft. When put back in the warrior's fist, it would always come to rest at its midpoint.

A crescent-shaped nose ornament, nearly identical to the two full-sized ones found nearby, swung freely from the septum of the warrior's nose. Minute crescent-shaped bells swayed from his belt. On his wrist was a removable circular shield, and on his head, an elaborate headdress with a large golden crescent. His ears were adorned with circular ear ornaments of gold and turquoise.

Around his neck lay a removable necklace of tiny beads, each minutely crafted to depict an owl head similar to the owl-head beads from the looted tomb (Fig. 44). At such a small scale, it seems impossible that the goldsmith who made these beads would have been able to perforate them for stringing. Yet in seeming disregard for the difficulty of the task, he followed the custom of double stringing — perforating the beads with four holes and then threading *two* strands of extremely fine gold wire through each!

The goldsmith's amazing virtuosity was further revealed in the anatomical detail of the warrior's limbs. Each knuckle was visible on his diminutive gold fist, as was the musculature of his forearm, thighs, and calves.

On these ornaments the central warrior was flanked by profile warriors, each with a circular shield and ear ornaments, and wearing an elaborate headdress. They too, were superbly crafted of turquoise and gold.

These extraordinary ear ornaments had been built up on a circular backing of wood (Fig. 88). A sheet of gold formed a background for the warrior. This background was surrounded by a band of turquoise mosaic and a separate gold ring with hollow gold spheres edge-welded to its periphery. These are certainly among the finest pieces of ancient jewelry ever found. Only under a magnifying glass can one appreciate the exacting craftsmanship wrought by their creator.

Once the nose ornaments and ear ornaments were removed from the tomb, we began excavating the area over the individual's head. The lower part of the face was covered by a large object of sheet gold hammered into the shape of cheeks, chin, mouth, and upper neck (Figs. 89, 90). This was unlike anything known previously from museums and private collections, and did not resemble anything depicted in Moche art. The absence of perforations along its sides implied that it was not meant to be worn in life, but was made to be placed over the lower face of the deceased. When it was lifted (Fig. 91), we found a nose, a band of teeth, and two eyes of sheet gold that had been placed over these parts of the individual's face (Fig. 92). The golden nose was incised with a supernatural fanged

FIG. 89

The individual's head
and torso, covered with a
sumptuous array of jewelry
and ritual paraphernalia.

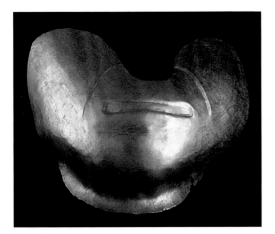

FIG. 90

(top) The sheet-gold object that covered the individual's lower face. W. 19.2 cms.

FIG. 91

(bottom) Over the individual's face were gold eyes, a nose, and a band of teeth.

FIG. 92

*Gold eyes W. 7.5 cms. each,
nose H. 8.5 cms., and band
of teeth W. 9 cms.*

face above two bird heads (Fig. 93). The golden band of teeth had a crude slit cut with a sharp chisel between the upper and lower teeth — perhaps as an afterthought. The golden eyes were open and appeared to be almost mirror images of one another. Close examination, however, revealed that there were subtle differences between them. The right eye, of nearly pure gold, was finely crafted and weighed 6.8 grams. The left eye was made of a gold-copper alloy that gave the piece a reddish hue. It was more crudely crafted than the right eye, and weighed only 4.5 grams. Was this a deliberate choice by the ancient artisan to make the two eyes different? Or were the two eyes made by different people, perhaps at different times? We may never know.

Traces of red pigment adhering to the frontal bone of the skull and around the eye orbits indicated that the deceased was wearing red face paint at the time of burial, a custom that has been noted in some other Moche burials, including those of men, women, and children. Near the head was a large circular band of gilded copper that may have been part of a headdress or crown, and a copper shaft which was part of a feathered headdress ornament.

The skull was resting on a shallow gold dish. It was oval at the rim, and had no decoration. It seemed very strange at first, since the Moche are not known to have made cups or plates of gold. Only later did we recall that more mundane Moche burials frequently have the head of the deceased resting in a shallow gourd plate, a simple, everyday object that in this extraordinarily elaborate burial had been replaced by a plate of hammered gold.

Around the neck of the deceased were three remarkable necklaces of hollow beads. The simplest consisted of gold spherical beads in graduated sizes (Fig. 94), almost identical to the spherical beads

FIG. 93

*Design incised on
the gold nose.*

91

FIG. 94

On the individual's chest were two ceremonial knives, and necklaces of peanut beads, spherical beads, and disc beads.

from the looted tomb (Fig. 26). The second necklace was composed of human-head beads, each crafted of sheet silver (Fig. 95). Finally, there was a spectacular necklace of gold and silver beads in the shape of peanuts (Figs. 94, 96) which, in size and form, were strikingly similar to the four peanut beads from the looted tomb (Fig. 27).

When the looted peanut beads were first brought to the Bruning Museum in 1987, we speculated at great length about how they originally had been strung. The fact that they had been torn from their original context left us so hopelessly distanced from the Moche jewelers who had strung them that it seemed unlikely we would ever know what the original necklace, or necklaces, looked like.

Now that we had found nearly identical beads in their original context, a necklace unlike *any* we had postulated was before us. It consisted of *two* strands, each with ten beads — five of gold and five of silver (Fig. 96). The gold peanuts began over the right shoulder of the wearer, and continued to the center of his chest. There the silver beads began, and they continued up over the left shoulder. The beads on the lower strand were larger than those on the upper strand. In this way each large peanut bead was paired with one of the same metal, but of smaller size. Between each pair of beads was a metal spacer bar which connected the two strands and held them in position.[6] The result was a magnificent necklace, balanced in elegant harmony, with each side forming the complement of the other.

All the hollow metal beads, with the exception of the spheres, had four perforations, and

FIG. 95

Necklace of silver human-head beads. H. 4 cms. each.

had been strung with two parallel cotton strings. This double stringing insured that the necklaces would not come apart if one of the strings broke. It also kept the beads from turning and twisting, and thus maintained their position relative to one another even as they shifted with the movement of the wearer.

In addition to the extraordinary necklaces of hollow beads, there was a necklace consisting of sixteen gold discs, each approximately 4.5 centimeters in diameter (Fig. 97). Each disc was perforated with two holes near one part of the edge. The discs are almost identical to the silver disc from the looted tomb (Fig. 36), strongly implying that a necklace of silver discs had been torn apart when that tomb was plundered.

---

[6] The large silver peanut bead from the looted tomb (Fig. 27) had a thin piece of silver attached to one end. We thought it might be part of the original peanut — perhaps meant to represent the stem. Now we realize that it is simply one of the metal rods that had been used to join the two strands of beads on the original necklace. It had become attached to one end of the peanut by a heavy layer of corrosion that covered both the peanut and the rod.

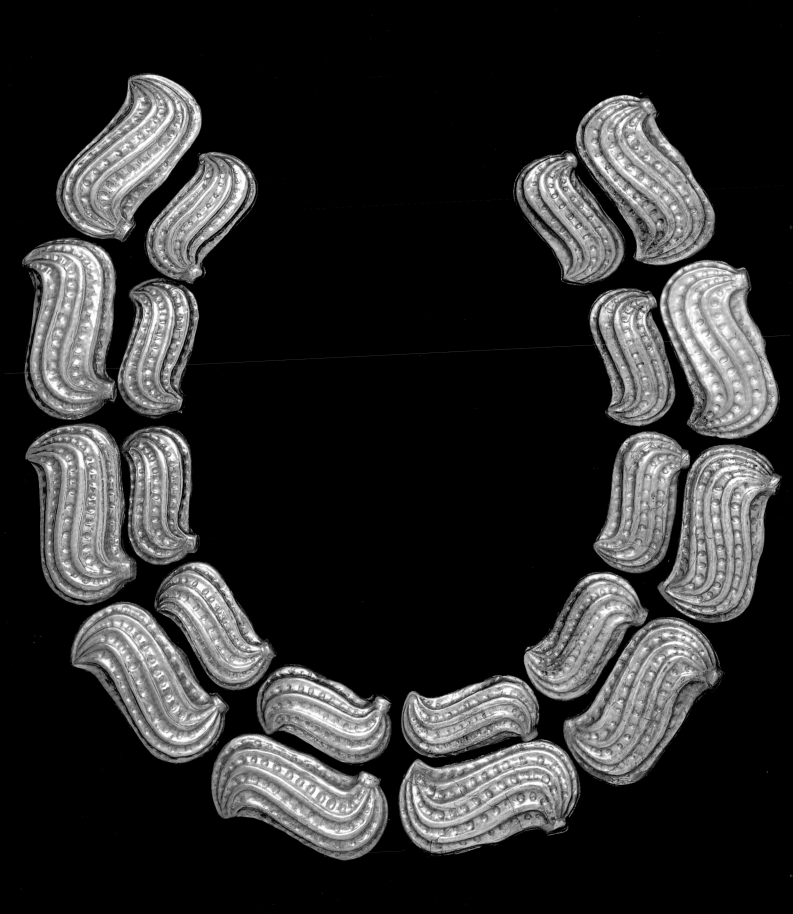

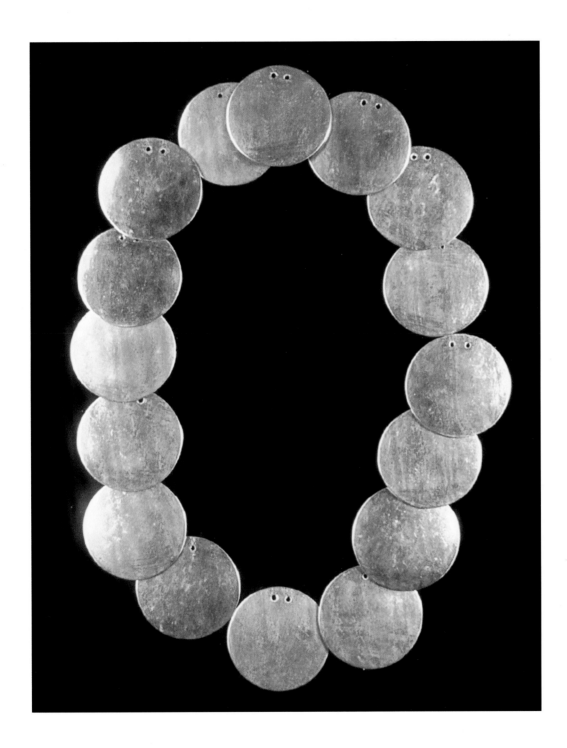

OPPOSITE PAGE:

FIG. 96
————

*Necklace of
gold and silver
peanut beads.
Largest 9 cms.
long.*

THIS PAGE:

FIG. 97
————

*Necklace of
gold discs.
Dia. 4.5 cms.
each.*

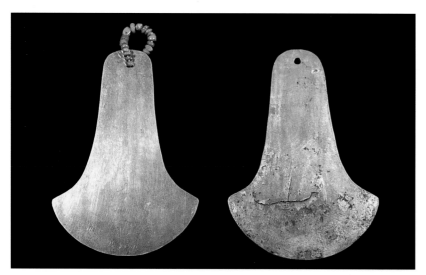

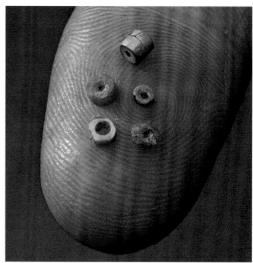

(left) A gold
H. 11.5 cms.
and a silver
H. 12 cms.
ceremonial
knife.

FIG. 99

(right) Tiny
gold, shell, and
stone beads.

Two ceremonial knives rested on the man's chest, one gold and the other silver (Figs. 94, 98). Such knives, known as *tumis*, are frequently depicted in Moche art. The narrow part of the knife is the handle, and the wider part at the bottom is the cutting edge. The top of the handle normally is perforated and has a loop of cordage through it.

In Moche art, *tumis* are used to cut off heads. Could it be that the individual buried in this coffin had been involved in decapitation ceremonies?

The gold *tumi* had a loop of cordage with a series of turquoise beads strung on it (Fig. 98). Near the silver *tumi* were five beads that may have been strung on its cordage. One of these was amethyst, two were sodalite, and two were tiny, hollow, cylindrical gold beads, made in two halves that were edge-welded at the center of their length (Fig. 99). The latter were identical to the tiny cylindrical gold beads from the looted tomb (Fig. 28). They are so small that it is difficult to imagine how they could have been crafted by the ancient metalsmiths.

As we cleared the area around the man's lower arms and hands, we found that both wrists wore exquisitely crafted beaded bracelets made of hundreds of minute turquoise, shell, and gold beads strung with copper spacer bars (Figs. 100, 101). These recalled the beaded bracelets worn by the men depicted on the banners excavated earlier (Figs. 60, 61, 62).

The right hand of the deceased grasped a large gold and silver scepter (Fig. 101), while the left hand held a smaller scepter of cast silver. Both objects were of the finest workmanship, and symbolically alluded to the role the individual had played in life. The large scepter had a trapezoidal, box-like chamber, superbly crafted of sheet gold (Fig. 102). The top of its chamber (Fig. 103) displayed a low relief scene: a nude prisoner sat cross-legged before an elaborately garbed warrior who appeared to thrust a warclub at the captive's head. The warrior wore a feathered headdress, a

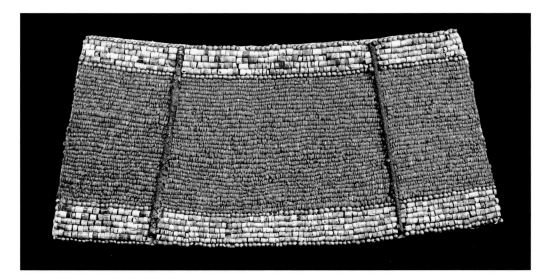

FIG. 100

(top) One of
the beaded
bracelets,
cleaned and
reconstructed.
W. 21 cms.

FIG. 101

(bottom)
Gold and silver
scepter in situ.

tunic, a belt, and a loincloth, as well as circular ear ornaments and a decorative nose ornament. He had a circular shield on his left wrist. The prisoner appeared to be restrained by a smaller, less elaborate warrior who held the prisoner's hair and arm. Above the small warrior was the captive's headdress. In the background were two birds that frequently appear in Moche combat scenes.[7] Each of the chamber's four sides displayed the same low relief scene, which was an abbreviated version of the scene on the top of the scepter. In the scene on the sides, the small warrior and the captive's head-dress were missing, and the large warrior held the prisoner by the hair.

These low relief designs explicitly depicted an elaborately dressed warrior subjugating the vanquished opponent. In each case, the warrior appeared to be the same individual, as though

[7] The presence of these birds may be an artistic canon to imply the swiftness of the warrior's movement, analogous to the swift darting back and forth that characterizes birds in flight.

FIG. 102

———

(left) Gold
and silver
scepter
cleaned.
H. 34.1 cms.

FIG. 103

———

(right) Top of
the scepter
chamber.
W. 12 cms.

the scepter was meant to commemorate the function of a specific person. It was intriguing to note that on all four sides and the top, the mouth of this individual had been opened with a sharp chisel cut, similar to the opening of the gold teeth band that lay over the mouth of the lord buried holding this scepter. Perhaps we were witnessing the lord himself, exquisitely depicted in gold on his own scepter.

At the bottom of the scepter's chamber was a gold tube, into which the upper part of a cast silver handle was inserted. The handle was itself an impressive work of art (Figs. 104a, b). It had a simple spatula blade at its lower end, but the upper part of the handle was decorated with military paraphernalia. On the front (Fig. 104a) there was a conical helmet with a crescent-shaped headdress ornament and an elaborate chin strap, a shirt, a circular shield, and a warrior's backflap. The latter, known from many examples in Moche

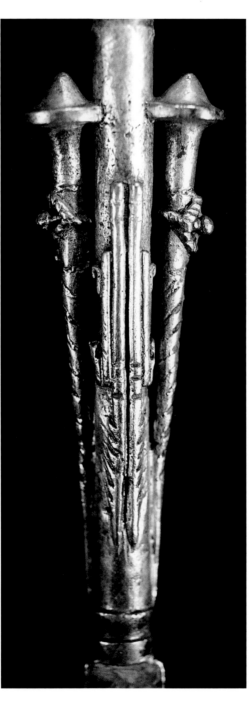

FIG. 104A
_____

(left) Detail of
the front of the
scepter handle.

FIG. 104B
_____

(right) Detail of
the back of the
scepter handle.

FIG. 105

Silver and
gold scepter.
H. 22 cms.

art, was a large metal ornament worn suspended from the back of a warrior's belt. On the two sides of the handle were warclubs with slings wrapped around them. In the diamond-shaped pocket of each sling was a sling stone. On the back of the handle (Fig. 104b) were spear throwers and spears.

The scepter (Fig. 105) held in the left hand of the deceased had an elaborate finial at its upper end (Fig. 106) and a long handle flattened to an edge at its lower end. The finial depicted an elegantly attired figure wearing a large crescent-shaped headdress, standing in front of a smaller kneeling figure with a rope around his neck.

It is clear that the motifs depicted on both the chamber and handle of the large scepter alluded to militarism, combat, and the treatment of prisoners. The latter was also the subject of the scene depicted on the small scepter. As will be seen below, these objects, held in the hands of the deceased, were to provide important clues to the identity and the ceremonial role this person played in Moche society.

We found a large gold ingot on the back of the downturned right hand, and an equally large silver ingot in the upturned left hand. Later, we found another large gold ingot in the mouth. In Moche burials it was customary to place copper ingots, or pieces of copper, in the hands and the mouth of the deceased. The large gold and silver ingots in this tomb appear to be an extraordinary elaboration of this custom.

FIG. 106

Detail of the
scepter finial.

101

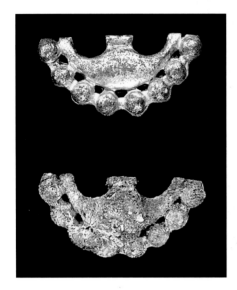

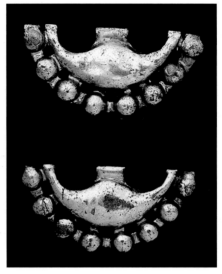

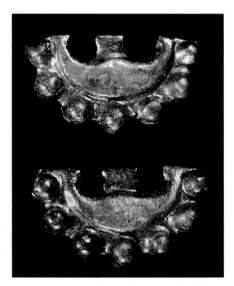

Near the individual's left shoulder were three pairs of gilded copper ornaments (Figs. 107, 108, 109). They appeared to be miniature bells, since they were made like the crescent bell from the looted tomb (Fig. 34), with small pellets in each of the spheres around their lower edge. At first we were unable to determine how these objects may have functioned. Only later did we realize that they were the ornaments seen at the ends of long ribbons hanging from elaborate Moche headdresses (Fig. 103).

Above the individual's waist were two gilded silver tweezers (Fig. 110) which were probably used for plucking whiskers. Silver sandals (Fig. 111) were attached to the feet with cotton straps. The sandals were rigid, and walking with them on would have been extremely awkward. Perhaps they were merely symbolic, or meant to be worn by the noble while carried in a litter.

Near the feet were two copper serpent heads — probably the ends of an elaborate belt or sash that has since decomposed (Figs. 112, 113). Moche art frequently illustrates high status adult males, as well as certain supernatural creatures, wearing double-headed serpent belts. There was a long pointed copper implement (Fig. 114) near the left leg. Although we can only speculate about its function, it may have been used as a dagger.

Small fragments of textile adhering to some of the metal objects suggested that the individual was wearing clothing at the time of burial. The garment, or garments, covered the upper body and the upper part of the legs. They appear to have been white with a complex design woven into them using an intricate manipulation of white warps and wefts.

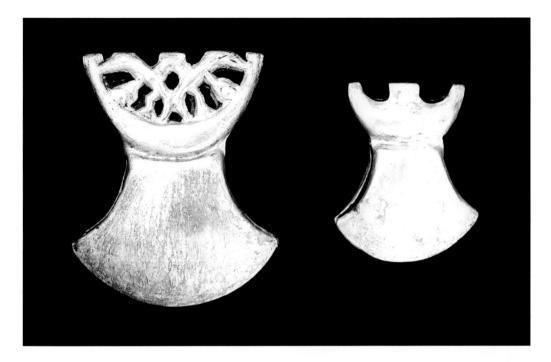

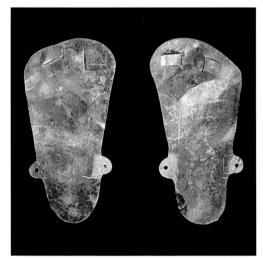

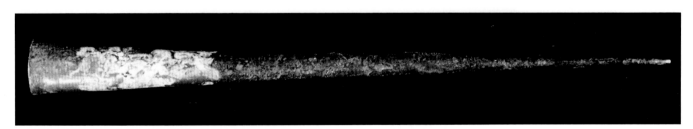

FIG. 110

(top) Gilded
silver tweezers.
Left, H. 4.2 cms.,
right, H. 6 cms.

FIG. 111

(far left)
Silver sandals.
H. 23.4 cms.

FIGS. 112, 113

(near left)
Copper belt finials.
L. 4.5 cms.

FIG. 114

(bottom)
Copper dagger.
L. 25.5 cms.

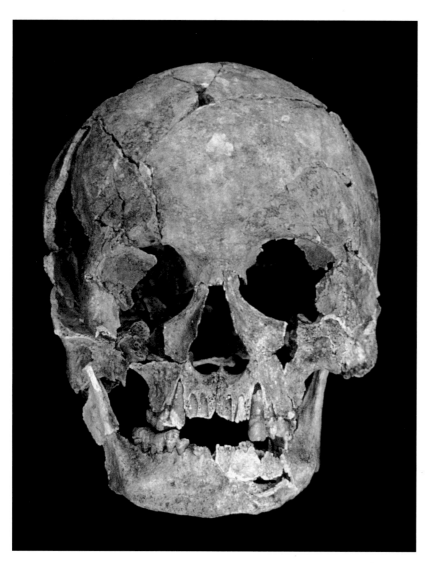

FIG. 115A

The individual's skull.

At this point in the excavation, most of the skeleton was visible. Unfortunately, the bones were in poor condition. Most were broken by the crushing weight of the soil that had pressed down on the tomb as the roof beams and coffin planks slowly decomposed. This destruction was compounded by the moisture in the tomb over many centuries which had caused the bones partially to decompose. They became friable when our excavation exposed them to the dry air, and tended to shatter into thousands of splintery fragments.

We decided that the best way to preserve the bones was to impregnate them with soluble resin when they were first exposed — a painstaking procedure at best, but one which solidified them into a single matrix. They could then be lifted out of the coffin by slipping wood slats beneath them. Fortunately, we were able to remove most of the skeleton in this way, making it available for study.

John Verano, a physical anthropologist from the Smithsonian Institution, was at the site to examine the bones *in situ* and to conduct additional analysis of them after they were transported to the museum. He also reconstructed the individual's skull (Fig. 115a), which had been crushed, and made an assessment of age, sex, and pathology. Verano concluded that the individual was a male, between thirty-five and forty-five years old at the time he died. He was about 166 centimeters (five feet five inches) tall, which is near the upper end of the height range for Moche males. He was probably thought of as tall. His bones were fairly delicate, and did not show signs of heavy muscle development. Overall, there are no indications that he was in poor health, although his back may have stiffened a bit from incipient arthritis. The back of his skull was flattened (Fig. 115b), a condition that is commonly seen on Moche skulls. The flattening was almost certainly caused by the practice of tying babies to their cradleboards or flat cane frames (Verano ms.b).

The man's lower-left second molar had a small cavity, but otherwise his teeth were in good condition and showed little wear. This contrasts with other Moche adults, who by their early thirties normally had several cavities, were missing teeth, and had severe tooth abrasion. In some instances the surfaces of their molars were ground down well beneath the enamel cortex. It would appear that this individual had a better diet, or perhaps simply ate food that was carefully prepared so that it did not contain much abrasive material (*ibid.*).

The cause of death could not be determined, although we can rule out poor diet and prolonged bone-damaging or deforming diseases. We can also rule out severe blows to the head or body that would have fractured the bones. He may have died rather suddenly from an illness or epidemic. It should be noted, however, that the average life expectancy for Moche males

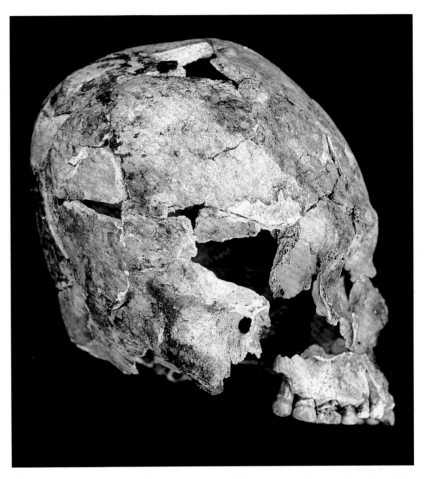

FIG. 115B

The individual's skull.

FIG. 116

When the skeleton was removed, a large gold headdress ornament was revealed.

was approximately thirty-five years of age (Verano 1990, ms.a, ms.b). This man's death, in his late thirties or early forties, would not have been unusual.

When the man's bones were lifted out of the coffin, a huge gold headdress ornament was revealed (Figs. 116, 117). More than sixty centimeters across, this spectacular crescent-shaped object mirrored the sun's rays in its polished gold surface. Riveted to the center of its base was a copper shaft, used to attach it to a conical helmet.

Partially covering the gold headdress ornament were feather bundles, each attached to a copper shaft (Figs. 117, 118). These had also been used as headdress ornaments. The feathers were almost completely decomposed, but an organic residue adhering to the surface of the adjacent metal objects gave some evidence of their original size and form.

Fortunately, John O'Neil, an ornithologist from the University of Louisiana and an expert on the birds of western South America, was in Peru at this time. We made arrangements for him to visit Sipán in the hope that he might be able to identify the birds from which the feathers had been taken. This identification was of great interest to us since it would allow us to reconstruct the original form and color of the feathers.

Although the feathers were badly decomposed, at least one species of bird could be identified. It

FIG. 117

*Large gold
headdress
ornament
in situ.
W. 62.7 cms.*

FIG. 118

Decomposed feathers found above the large gold headdress ornament.

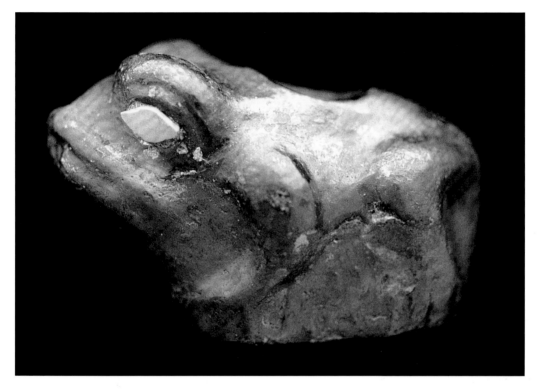

FIG. 119

*Copper
frog with
turquoise
eyes.
L. 2.6 cms.*

was the Chilean flamingo (family Phoenicopteridae), a bird known to inhabit the lakes and lagoons of the Andean cordillera, as well as the marshy tidelands that form at the deltas of some rivers along the coast. O'Neil felt fairly certain that they were axillary feathers from under the wing, or covert feathers from the upper part of its wing. Both types of feathers are a medium coral red.

When the feathered headdress ornaments and the large gold crescent were removed, we found a small copper frog with turquoise eyes (Fig. 119). It was near the right side of the base of the gold headdress ornament. The opening in the upper part of its back suggests that it may have been an ocarina.

Beneath the frog and large gold headdress ornament was a thin rectangular mass of brown organic residue. Careful cleaning with air squeeze bulbs and examination with magnifying lenses indicated that it was fibrous material — the decomposed remains of parallel wood slats that had been tied together. In some simpler Moche burials, the body was kept rigid by laying it on a cane frame and wrapping the body and frame in a textile shroud. The frame of wood slats in this burial appears to have been analogous to the cane frames in simpler burials.[8]

Beneath the wood frame was an ensemble of spectacular jewelry consisting of two elaborate gilded

---

[8] One piece of the wood frame was sufficiently well preserved that it could be radiocarbon dated. This provided a date of A.D. 260 ± 90 years (Beta 23147), a date that we feel accurately reflects the age of this burial.

FIG. 120

Two gilded
copper bells
and a gold
and a silver
backflap
in situ.

FIG. 121

copper bells and two large warrior backflaps (Fig. 120). The bells (Fig. 121) are almost identical to the one from the looted tomb that was confiscated by the police (Fig. 35), but they have a much more animated and powerful appearance because their original inlay is in place. They are also similar to the bells that hang from the belts of the tiny warriors on the warrior ear ornaments (Figs. 86, 87, 88).

Gilded copper bell. H. 11 cms.

The backflaps (Figs. 122, 123) are objects unique to the Moche, and apparently were worn only by warriors. Normally, a person wore only one, suspended from the back of his belt so that the large, flaring edge hung down. Both backflaps in this tomb were made of single sheets of metal, one of gold and the other of silver. The upper part of each was crafted like the bells, with the same deity figure, and spheres containing sound-producing copper pellets.

The two backflaps are among the most spectacular objects in the tomb. They are forty-five centimeters high, and the one of gold weighs nearly one kilogram. It is the largest and heaviest Moche gold object known today. It must have been an extremely impressive, and probably famous, object to these ancient people.

Both the bells and the backflaps carry the same decoration — a frontal figure with a large fanged mouth who holds a human head by the hair in one hand, and a *tumi* in the other. His eyes, mouth, and ears are inlaid with shell and semiprecious stones. These inlays greatly enhance the power and

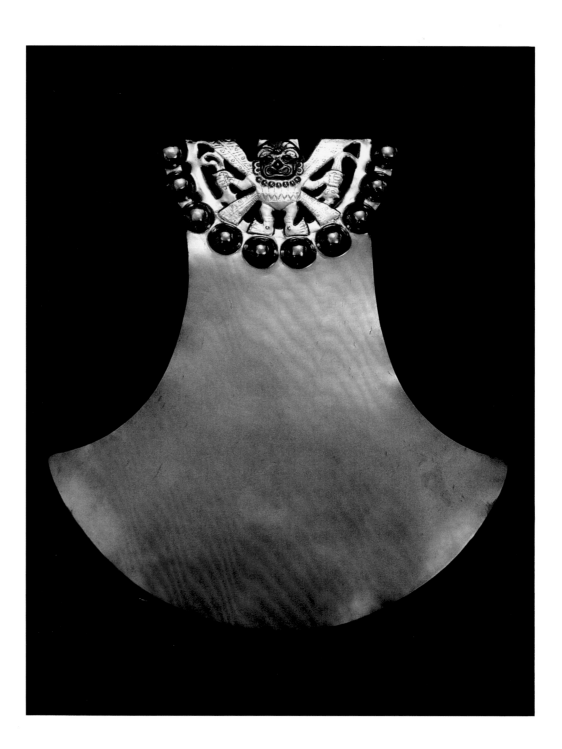

FIG. 122

Gold backflap.
H. 45 cms.

FIG. 123

Silver backflap.
H. 45.5 cms.

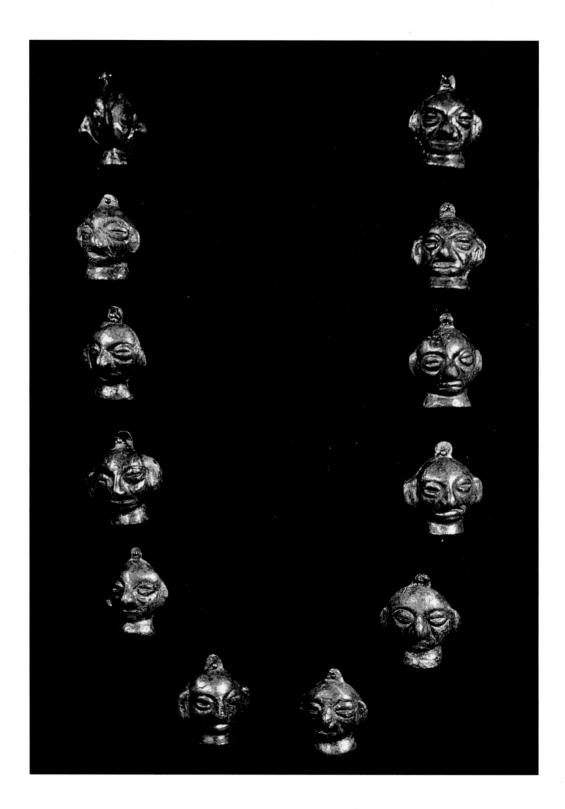

FIG. 124

Necklace of
gilded copper
Janus-head
beads.
H. 3.5 cms.
each.

spiritual quality of the objects; the mouths take on a ferocious snarling appearance, and the eyes stare forward menacingly beneath heavy eyelids.

When the bells and backflaps were removed, we found another gilded copper necklace of human-head beads (Fig. 124). These had opposing faces, neck-like pedestals, and a loop at the top of the head for suspension instead of the customary holes at the sides for stringing.

Beneath these beads, we found another group of pectorals. Once again, the excavation was delayed while we went through the painstaking process of cleaning and removing each pectoral so that it could later be reconstructed. Three of the pectorals were of white shell beads; the fourth combined white and pink shell beads to create broad horizontal stripes similar to those on one of the pectorals previously excavated.

Beneath the pectorals were two more banners. Like those found in the upper part of the coffin, squares of cloth had been covered on one side with male figures and rectangular platelets of gilded copper, and a row of gilded copper cones had been sewn along the bottom hem. In these instances, however, the sides covered with metal were facing down instead of up. Furthermore, the two banners had been sewn together, the top edge of one overlapping the bottom edge of the other to create a single rectangular panel. Three narrow copper straps had been sewn along its back side. The purpose of sewing the banners together and adding the copper straps is not known, but it may have facilitated raising them together at some ceremonial occasion.

When the banners were removed, other objects similar to those at the top of the coffin were found. These included another headdress with an elaborate chin strap, and five more feathered headdress ornaments. There was also another necklace of hollow gilded copper beads in the form of human heads.

Certain types of objects found near the top of the coffin were duplicated as we approached its bottom. There also appears to have been a tendency to place some object types close to the body, both above and below it. This, coupled with the fact that the upper banners were facing up and the lower banners were facing down, suggests that the loading of the coffin was deliberately done in such a way that the body was *sandwiched between* the same sequence of layered objects, both above and below it.

FIG. 125

*Small gold
headdress
ornament.
W. 26.9 cms.*

Near the head of the coffin there was a crescent-shaped headdress ornament of sheet gold (Fig. 125), smaller than the one found beneath the body (Fig. 117), but of similar form. Its narrow base was incised with a depiction of the same figure shown on the bells and backflaps (Fig. 126). A copper shaft was riveted to the base for attachment to a headdress. Adjacent to this gold ornament was another elaborate chin strap and a final feathered headdress ornament.

One broad copper strap was found at the foot of the coffin. Its function remains an enigma, though possibly it served as part of a metal crown.

At this level we found additional remains of the three burial shrouds that were first encountered at the top of the coffin: the inner shroud with square platelets, the middle one with round platelets, and the outer shroud with its characteristic red color. Along the sides and foot of the coffin, near the floor, were numerous sea shells. They were exclusively of two types: *Spondylus* spp. and *Conus fergusonii*, neither of which inhabits the coast of northern Peru. They had been imported from the warm tropical ocean off the coast of Ecuador.

FIG. 126

Design incised on the base of the small gold headdress ornament.

Finally, at the bottom of the coffin were three miniature warclubs and shields made of sheet copper, and a bundle of copper spearpoints. The way these points were stacked in one corner near the foot of the coffin suggested that they had been hafted to cane or wood spear shafts which had long since decomposed. Spears of this type were thrown with a spear thrower. Perhaps a spear thrower made of perishable material had also been included in the coffin, but had deteriorated beyond recognition.

Careful cleaning revealed the three broad planks that comprised the floor of the coffin. The outer two were tied to the side and end planks with copper strapping. There is no evidence, however, that the center plank was tied to any other. This suggests that the plank coffin was assembled on the floor of the funerary chamber and was never meant to be moved as a unit. It would simply have been filled with its remarkable contents *in situ* and closed with the three planks that formed its lid. It appears that all three of the lid planks were securely tied shut with copper straps.

With the cleaning of the floor planks, the coffin was finally empty. We had been excavating continuously, six days each week for nearly six months, the last four months of which were devoted to

FIG. 127

Burial chamber with the remains of the plank coffin in the center of the floor.

this grave. Though exhausted by the strain of meticulous cleaning, drawing, photographing, and removing these objects one by one for so many weeks and months, we were spurred on by the fascination of what had been found, and profoundly gratified by the remarkable archaeological data that were resulting from our work. The project had settled into a basic routine, where all involved knew their responsibilities and had long since adjusted to their roles as part of the excavation team.

The project itself had evolved from a short-term salvage excavation into a major archaeological field program. Our meager starting funds were exhausted after the first few months. A brewery then provided partial funding, and a pasta manufacturer in Chiclayo donated a truckload of noodles to the project. At one point we were paying the field workers with a combination of cash and noodles. As these resources were being depleted, we approached the Research Committee of the National Geographic Society. They provided the funds necessary to maintain the project, and to ensure that we had the equipment and personnel needed to continue.

With firm financial support, we were able to construct living quarters for the archaeologists and police guards, as well as laboratory facilities for preliminary cleaning and conservation of the objects prior to their shipment to the museum. Thus the project was secure, and our attention could be fully devoted to the excavation of the tomb.

For months, as the contents of the plank coffin were being excavated, we had been working and moving equipment around all four of its sides. We had absolutely no idea that we had been walking only centimeters above hundreds of ceramic vessels, and the burials of six other individuals!

Over the next six months, we painstakingly excavated these remains. Only then did we understand the full complexity of the remarkable tomb, and the nature of its construction. The burial chamber was actually a room, with solid mud-brick benches along its sides and at the head end. Niches had been created in these benches — two in each of the sides and one at the head (Fig. 127). The benches reduced the floor space of the burial chamber to an area 2.40 meters north-south by 3.25 meters east-west. The plank coffin had been placed in the center of this area, aligned parallel to the side walls. The contents of the coffin were then placed inside it, and the coffin lid was securely fastened with copper straps.

Hundreds of ceramic vessels were subsequently lowered into the burial chamber and arranged in groups that filled the niches in the side benches. Some ceramics were also placed on the floor near the head of the coffin, and along the right and left sides of the interred lord (Figs. 127, 128).

FIG. 128

Ceramic jars in a niche at the side of the burial chamber.

FIG. 129

*Niche at
the head of
the burial
chamber.*

The ceramics were predominantly mold-made jars, sculpted in the form of nude prisoners with ropes around their necks, warriors holding warclubs and shields, and seated figures with their hands on their knees or chests. Most were neither painted nor polished, and appear to have been mass-produced (Fig. 128). They were remarkably similar to those found in Offering 1.

Somewhat finer ceramics were placed in the niche at the head of the burial (Fig. 129). These included stirrup spout bottles in the form of seated humans, owls, and lizards. This selection presumably meant something special to the Moche people, but its meaning is unknown to us today. In one side niche, there was a fragmented stirrup spout bottle depicting a seated figure with inlaid eyes and copper ear ornaments (Fig. 130).

At about the time the ceramics were being placed in the burial chamber, two sacrificed llamas were put on the floor — one on each side adjacent to the foot of the coffin (Fig. 127). The body of a child was also placed on the floor near the head of the coffin. The child was seated with its back leaning against the southwest corner of the burial chamber, and its legs extended forward along the floor.

The child had died at age nine or ten.[9] The dentition suggests several episodes of either illness or dietary deficiency from which the child had recovered, but which left a permanent record in the developing tooth crowns. A cavity in the deciduous upper second molar also suggests that this child may have been in poor health (Verano ms.b).

Once the ceramics, llamas, and child were placed in the funerary chamber, five cane coffins, each containing one adult, were lowered into position. One of these coffins, containing the body of an

---

[9] It is not possible to determine the gender of such a young child by analysis of the skeleton.

FIG. 130

Ceramic bottle from a niche at the side of the burial chamber.

FIG. 131

Burial
chamber
with the
burials that
were placed
around the
plank coffin.

adult male, was placed on the east side of the plank coffin, directly on top of one of the sacrificed llamas (Fig. 131). The body was fully extended, lying on its back with the head to the south. The left foot was missing. The man was between thirty-five and fifty years old at the time he died (Verano ms.b). Although shorter in stature than the lord in the plank coffin, he was more powerfully built, with a massive square chin and large teeth. His body was covered with copper objects, including a large crescent-shaped headdress ornament and a circular shield. Alongside his body was a large war-club, completely encased in copper sheet. His body had been wrapped in a coarsely woven shroud, and placed inside a rectangular box-like coffin made of cane.

On the other side of the plank coffin was another cane coffin, placed on top of the other sacrificed llama. It also contained an adult male lying extended on his back (Fig. 131). In this instance, however, the head was to the north. His age at death has been estimated as between thirty-five and

FIG. 132
———
(top) Copper headdress worn by the female at the foot of the plank coffin. H. 13 cms.

FIG. 133
———
(bottom) Original appearance of the copper headdress shown in Figure 132.

forty-five years (*ibid*.). He was wearing a beaded pectoral, and had several unidentified copper objects on top of his body. Inside his coffin was a dog, stretched out with its head near the man's feet and its tail by the man's waist.

Three other cane coffins contained adult females. Two of these were stacked one on top of the other at the head of the plank coffin. The lower coffin had been placed over the extended legs of the child seated in the southwest corner of the burial chamber. Both females were fully extended with their heads to the east. The lower individual lay on her back, while the upper one was lying face down.

The third cane coffin containing a female was at the foot of the plank coffin. She lay on her side with her head to the west, facing the plank coffin.

All three women were between fifteen and twenty years old when they died (*ibid*.). They exhibited no sign of illness or violent death, but the upper female at the head of the plank coffin was missing her left foot. These women had relatively few objects in their coffins, although the woman at the foot of the plank coffin was buried wearing a large copper headdress (Figs. 132, 133), and the upper individual at the head of the plank coffin was wearing a beaded pectoral.

As the burials around the plank coffin were being excavated, we thought they were individuals who had been sacrificed in order to accompany the principal figure in the afterlife. Perhaps the flanking males were his bodyguards, or members of his court, and the females were his wives, concubines, or servants.

While this supposition may be valid concerning the males, we were to learn that it may not have been true for the females. Their skeletal

FIG. 134

*Burial chamber
as it might have
appeared at the
time of the funeral.*

remains suggest that they had died long before the principal figure, and that their bodies were partially decomposed at the time they were put in his tomb. Their bones were disarticulated and jumbled in ways that could not have occurred with *in situ* decomposition of the bodies (*ibid.*). This was most apparent in the torso, where the ribs and vertebrae were completely out of position. This state suggests that the bodies were placed in the burial chamber *after* substantial soft tissue decomposition, when the bones were free to move about inside the textile wrappings that formed the burial shrouds.

We do not know how long the women had been dead prior to their placement in the royal tomb. They may have died during the life of the principal male, although it is also possible that they had been dead long before he was born. Whatever the case, their bodies were probably wrapped in burial shrouds, placed in cane coffins, and subsequently stored in a dry, sheltered place for many years while the soft tissue decomposed, freeing the ribs and vertebrae. This may have occurred in a palace, or in a temple at the summit of one of the pyramids.[10] Then, on the occasion of the death of someone of the importance of the principal male, they were brought out of storage for placement in his tomb. The movement involved in transporting these bodies to the grave site, lowering them into the funerary chamber, and putting them into their final resting place would have caused the bones to fall out of position.

With the coffins in place, the tomb was sealed by the construction of the beam roof. The roof was only slightly higher than the benches that extended along the sides and head of the burial chamber, and would have been only a little more than a meter above the floor — too low to have created a room in which people could have stood upright.

The roof was covered with soil as the area above it was filled. It was in this fill, approximately fifty centimeters above the roof, that the footless first male burial had been located (Fig. 134).

High up on the south wall of the chamber, approximately one meter above the roof beams, there was one final burial. The body was seated with its legs crossed and its hands on its knees. It had been placed in a small niche, carved into the south wall, so that it looked out over the royal mausoleum. And so it had remained, undisturbed, for seventeen centuries.

---

[10] Early accounts of the native people in the Andean area report that the bodies of certain stillborn infants were kept in households as sacred objects (Arriaga 1968:31). In a similar fashion, it may be that the bodies of these women had been kept as sacred objects prior to burial.

FIG. 135
_____

Kneeling warrior.
H. 25.3 cms.

MOCHE WARFARE AND THE SACRIFICE OF PRISONERS

▼ As Tomb 1 was being excavated and its contents catalogued, one question kept recurring to all who participated: "Who was this person?" Analysis of the bones indicated an adult male about forty years of age. The elaborate tomb, with its unusual plank coffin, accompanying male and female burials, and the quantity and quality of grave goods, attested to an individual of high status — a member of the nobility. But a more precise identification of this noble and the role he played in Moche society was possible only through a careful study of Moche art.

The key to this research was a major photographic archive of Moche art, located on the campus of the University of California in Los Angeles (UCLA). This archive, containing more than 125,000 photographs of Moche objects in museums and private collections throughout the world, has served for many years as an important resource for the study of Moche culture. As the tomb was being excavated, photographs of the objects were sent to UCLA for comparative study.

If we assume that the objects in the plank coffin were worn and used by the man during his lifetime, they should tell us about his role in Moche society. Many of the objects in his coffin suggest that he was a warrior. Warriors and warrior activities were very frequently depicted by Moche artists, and the archive of Moche art contains hundreds of these depictions that can be grouped into categories forming a sequential narrative of Moche militarism and the ceremonial activities that follow it.

There are many sculptural depictions of warriors, generally kneeling (Fig. 135) or standing and holding warclubs diagonally across their chests. Some fineline drawings show processions of warriors (Fig. 136), perhaps as they marched toward the field of battle. Others show warriors engaged in

FIG. 136

Procession of warriors carrying warclubs, spears, and spear throwers.

FIG. 137

_____

(top) Warriors
in combat.

FIG. 138

_____

(bottom) Warriors
defeating their
opponents.

FIG. 139

*Combat in
open terrain.*

combat (Figs. 137, 138, 139). The hills and plants depicted in some of these (Fig. 139) suggest that combat took place at some distance from Moche settlements, religious structures, canals, or even cultivated fields — presumably in the barren expanses of desert terrain that lie between fertile river valleys. In no instance are soldiers shown attacking a castle or fortified settlement, nor killing, capturing, or mistreating nonmilitary personnel. Moreover, there is no evidence that the Moche employed any equipment or tactics that involved teams of warriors acting in close coordination. We see no regular formations of troops like Greek phalanxes, or siege instruments whose operation would have involved trained squads of individuals.

Although there are a few depictions of two warriors fighting a single opponent, the essence of Moche warfare appears to have been the expression of *individual* valor in which the warriors engaged in one-on-one combat. In rare instances it is clear that one or more of the combatants was actually killed, but normally only the vanquishing of the enemy is shown. This generally involved hitting the opponent on the head or upper body with the warclub. Defeat is indicated by the enemy receiving such a blow, bleeding profusely from his nose, losing his headdress and possibly other parts of his attire, or by the victor grasping his hair, removing his nose ornament, or slapping his face.

FIG. 140

—————

(top) Parading
of prisoners.

FIG. 141

—————

(bottom)
Arraignment
of prisoners.

FIG. 142

Prisoners arriving at a ceremonial precinct for arraignment and sacrifice.

Once an enemy was defeated, some or all of his clothing was removed, a rope was placed around his neck, and his hands were sometimes tied behind his back. The prisoner's clothing and weapons were made into a weapon bundle[11] which was tied to the victor's warclub and slung over his shoulder (Fig. 140). The victor held the rope tied to the prisoner's neck and forced the prisoner to walk in front of him. The many fineline drawings of warriors with prisoners suggest that public parading and display of the spoils of war was an important part of Moche militarism.

The prisoners were ultimately taken to a place where they were formally arraigned before a high status individual (Fig. 141). At the arraignment, weapon bundles were often placed on the ground near the prisoners. The arraignment is sometimes shown in the setting of sandy hillsides, perhaps near the field of battle. The prisoners were brought back to Moche settlements or ceremonial precincts. One scene (Fig. 142) clearly shows them arriving at a large pyramid with a structure at its summit — a setting similar to the pyramids at Sipán.

---

[11] Weapon bundles are frequently depicted in Moche art. They are often shown as individual design motifs and frequently are animated with arms, legs, and a face.

FIG. 143

The Sacrifice Ceremony. Prisoner sacrifice (lower register) and consumption of blood (upper register).

Following arraignment there was a ceremony in which the prisoners were sacrificed by having their throats cut (Fig. 143 lower center and right) and their blood consumed by priests and attendants (Fig. 143 upper). The prisoners' bodies were then dismembered: their heads, hands, and feet were removed and tied individually with ropes to create trophies (Fig. 144).

It is clear that the primary objective of warfare was the capture of prisoners for sacrifice. Since the Sacrifice Ceremony is of special relevance to Tomb 1, and particularly to the identification of the principal person buried there, it is worthwhile to examine it in detail.

There are many representations of the Sacrifice Ceremony in Moche art, and these imply that it was an important aspect of Moche religion. In this respect, it is somewhat analogous to the many depictions of the Nativity in Christian art. Although the symbolic elements that characterize the Nativity are standard (the infant, Mary, wise men, manger, star, etc.), there is considerable variation in the way they are combined. Some representations show only the star or the infant, while others combine multiple elements in various ways. The complete inventory of elements, however, is rarely found in a single representation.

The same is true of the way Moche artists depicted the Sacrifice Ceremony. The symbolic elements that characterize it are standard, but there is considerable variation in the way they are combined. Some representations show only a single element; others involve combinations of multiple elements.

FIG. 144

Dismemberment of prisoners.

The Sacrifice Ceremony depiction in Figure 143 is one of the most complete. The four principal priests who participate in the Sacrifice Ceremony are in the upper register of this scene. Most important is the Warrior Priest, the large figure on the left, who holds a tall goblet. Rays emanate from his head and shoulders, and he wears a conical helmet with a crescent-shaped ornament at its peak, a crescent-shaped nose ornament, large circular ear ornaments, and a warrior backflap. A dog is adjacent to his feet.

The figure to the right of the Warrior Priest is the Bird Priest. He is always part bird and part human and is always shown wearing either a conical helmet (as in this representation) or a head-dress with an owl at its center (see below).

To the right of the Bird Priest is the Priestess, who always wears a dress-like garment and a head-dress with two prominent plumes. Her hair is in wrapped braids that hang down over her chest and end in serpent heads.

To the right of the Priestess is the fourth major participant, a priest who always wears a headdress with long streamers having serrated upper edges, and a sash-like garment with a fringe of discs at the end. His headdress is a half-circle of sheet metal with an animal face, perhaps a feline, embossed near its center. This half-circle is flanked by two curved pieces of sheet metal, and at the back of the headdress is a fan of feathers.

In the lower register of this scene two nude prisoners are having their throats cut. Their hands are tied behind their backs and their weapon bundles are placed to one side.

To the left of the prisoners is a litter with rays projecting from its backrest. This is the litter of the Warrior Priest who is seen in the register above. In other scenes the Warrior Priest is actually riding in the litter. Human heads hang from the ends of the litter poles, and a feline is perched in front of the seat. Above the feline and tied to the litter with a cord is a scepter, shown in horizontal view,

with its box-like chamber on the left and its spatula-bladed handle on the right.

There are a number of secondary figures and objects in this scene. Of particular relevance to Tomb 1 are the paisley-shaped fruits that appear to float in the background. These are called *ulluchus,* and have been identified as a member of the papaya family (Wassén 1985/86). Native people in the tropical forest of South America recognize the anticoagulant property of this fruit, and it is thought that the Moche may have used it to keep the human blood from coagulating during the Sacrifice Ceremony (*ibid.*). It is interesting that *ulluchus* are associated with two activities in Moche art that involve the ritual consumption of blood — the Sacrifice Ceremony and deer hunting (McClelland 1977). Deer are often anthropomorphized, sometimes as warriors or as prisoners with ropes around their necks. The ritual hunting of deer was clearly analogous to the capture and sacrifice of warriors (Donnan 1982).

FIG. 145

Prisoner sacrifice
(lower register)
and consumption
of blood
(upper register).

Figure 145 illustrates a somewhat simpler version of the Sacrifice Ceremony. It is a low relief design that decorates the bottom of a ceramic dipper. The Warrior Priest with his characteristic clothing and ornaments stands in the upper left. The Bird Priest faces him, holding a Sacrifice Ceremony goblet. Here he wears his more typical headdress, with an owl in the center and curved elements extending out to both sides. He also wears a prominent warrior backflap. The dog crouches between the Warrior Priest and the Bird Priest. In the lower register is a weapon bundle on the left, a bird warrior in the center, and a bound nude prisoner with a feline captor on the right. Another weapon bundle, presumably the prisoner's weapons and clothing, is in the center, and floating in the background of both the upper and lower registers are *ulluchus.*

A third depiction of the Sacrifice Ceremony, by yet another artist, is seen in Figure 146. Although portions of this scene have spalled off the bottle on which it is painted, it is easy to recognize the characteristic elements. The Warrior Priest, Bird Priest, and Priestess are in the upper register, along with the companion dog, *ulluchus,* and a weapon bundle. Above the weapon bundle is a bound prisoner having his blood taken by a feline captor. The lower register depicts the combat that preceded the Sacrifice Ceremony.

FIG. 146

Combat
(lower register)
and consumption
of blood
(upper register).

FIG. 147

(top) Gold ear ornaments with the Warrior Priest depicted on each. Dia. 7.6 cms.

FIG. 148

(near right) Ceramic figurine depicting the Priestess. H. 14.2 cms.

FIG. 149

(far right) Ceramic bottle depicting the Bird Priest. H. 24 cms.

Once we understand the cast of individuals and inventory of objects in the Sacrifice Ceremony, we are able to identify them even in simplified form. For example, there are depictions of the Warrior Priest on the front of a pair of gold ear ornaments (Fig. 147), and ceramic depictions of the Bird Priest (Fig. 149), the Priestess (Fig. 148), the bound prisoner with feline captor (Fig. 150), and even the companion dog (Fig. 151).

The Sacrifice Ceremony was clearly of great importance in the religion of the Moche people, and their artists, like Christian artists depicting

FIGS. 150 A, B

(top) Ceramic bottle depicting a prisoner and feline captor. H. 27.3 cms.

FIG. 151

(bottom) Ceramic bottle depicting the companion dog. H. 18.4 cms.

the Nativity, were able to manipulate, combine, or separate out its symbolic elements to create masterful works of art, each of which would have been perfectly recognizable to the Moche.

Understanding of Moche militarism and prisoner sacrifice enables us to recognize that nearly all of the objects in Tomb 1 relate directly to these activities, especially militarism, suggesting that the principal occupant of the tomb was not merely a warrior, but a warrior of great wealth and high status. Indeed, it appears likely that he was none other than the Warrior Priest.

Evidence of his warrior affiliation is abundant. The two backflaps (Figs. 122, 123) are clear evidence of his occupation, since only warriors wear backflaps. Other indications are the crescent bells normally worn on a warrior's belt (Fig. 121), the spear points, and the miniature sheet metal club and shield near the foot of the coffin.

Outside the plank coffin were many objects that further underscore the wealth and status of the principal figure and his association with military aspects of Moche culture. On each side of the principal figure were burials of adult males between thirty-five and fifty years of age. These individuals had been very muscular in life and may have been warriors. The man on the right side of the principal figure was buried with military equipment — a copper crescent-shaped headdress ornament, a copper shield, and a copper-covered warclub. The man on the left side of the principal figure had a dog buried with him inside his cane coffin. This may well have been the companion dog that frequently accompanies the Warrior Priest at the Sacrifice Ceremony (Figs. 143, 145, 146, 151).

Placed on the floor of the burial chamber and in niches built into its sides were numerous ceramic jars (Fig. 128), some of which depicted warriors holding shields and warclubs, and prisoners with ropes around their necks.

In addition to these objects indicating warrior affiliation, there are many iconographic referents to warriors and warfare. The scenes on the four sides and top of the scepter chamber (Figs. 102, 103) show a warrior vanquishing an enemy. The scepter handle (Figs. 104a, b) is decorated with military equipment — warclubs, slings with sling stones, a spear thrower with spears, a shield, a helmet, and a tunic. The finial on the other scepter (Figs. 105, 106) depicts a prisoner with rope around his neck seated before an elaborately dressed standing figure holding a warclub — a tableau clearly related to the arraignment of prisoners. One pair of ear ornaments (Fig. 87) depicts a frontal warrior holding a warclub, flanked by warriors in profile. His crescent headdress ornament, crescent nose ornament, large circular ear ornaments, and the pair of bells hanging from his belt are identical to objects found in the coffin of the principal figure in this tomb.

The two other pairs of ear ornaments found in Tomb 1 may also allude to a militaristic theme. In Moche art the duck is generally depicted in naturalistic form, either in three-dimensional ceramic sculpture or in fineline drawing. When not shown in natural form the duck is sometimes an anthropomorphized warrior who occasionally participates in the Sacrifice Ceremony. His appearance on the gold and turquoise ear ornaments in Tomb 1 (Fig. 85) may be related to his involvement in warfare and in the ceremony where prisoners of war were ritually slain. The motivation for depicting the deer on the other pair of gold and turquoise ear ornaments (Fig. 82) seems to relate to the Moche's ritual deer hunt, which was analogous to the capture of warriors on the field of battle.

The motif that decorates the crescent bells and warrior backflaps in Tomb 1 (Figs. 121, 122, 123) is yet another iconographic referent to human sacrifice and particularly to human decapitation. This design depicts the Decapitator, a supernatural figure who holds a crescent-bladed knife in one hand, with a rope-like lanyard curving up above his clenched fist. In his other hand he holds a human head by the hair. Recent research by Alana Cordy-Collins (1992) has demonstrated that the Decapitator is an anthropomorphized spider, and that the four elements radiating out from his torso are pairs of legs (Fig. 152). Spiders are an appropriate analog to warriors in Moche culture since spiders capture their prey, tie them with ropes of web, and later extract their vital fluids — just as Moche warriors captured the enemy, tied them with ropes, and later drank their blood (*ibid.*).

The crescent-bladed knife, which is used for decapitation, appears to have been limited to ceremonial use.[12] In this regard, it is interesting to note that the individual in the plank coffin was buried with two of these knives, one of gold and the other of silver (Fig. 98). These knives underscore his involvement in the decapitation of prisoners. One other referent to this theme is the large sheet metal figure of a headless human with outstretched hands (Fig. 66). The function of this object is unclear, but its iconography clearly reflects human decapitation.

FIG. 152

The relationship between the spider (left) and the Decapitator (center and right) in Moche art.

---

[12] It may also have been the instrument used to dismember prisoners after they were sacrificed.

FIG. 153

Gold and
silver scepter
from the
looted tomb
at Sipán.
H. 30.5 cms.

A final iconographic reference to warfare and sacrifice is the row of *ulluchus* shown in low relief around the borders of the banners (Fig. 62). As noted above, it has been suggested that *ulluchus* may have an anticoagulant property that would have been useful in keeping the blood in a fluid state during the Sacrifice Ceremony. The depiction of *ulluchus* on the banners in Tomb 1 thus alludes to the sacrifice ritual.

The objects in and around the plank coffin in Tomb 1 indicate strongly that the deceased was not only a warrior, but specifically the Warrior Priest — the principal figure at the ceremony where prisoners of war were sacrificed and their blood ritually consumed. As noted above, the Warrior Priest was consistently depicted wearing a conical helmet with a large crescent-shaped headdress ornament, large circular ear ornaments, large bracelets, and a warrior back-flap. He was frequently shown wearing a large crescent-shaped nose ornament (Fig. 143) and cones hanging as fringe from the hem of his tunic (Fig. 145). Each of these items was found inside the plank coffin.[13]

One more piece of evidence supports his identification as the Warrior Priest — the scepter which he was holding in his right hand (Fig. 102). This type of scepter was seldom depicted in Moche art, but existing examples clearly indi-

---

[13] The pattern of radiant triangles on one of the pectorals (Fig. 74) may have symbolized the rays that emanate from the head and shoulders of the Warrior Priest.

cate that it was part of the ritual paraphernalia used at the Sacrifice Ceremony. The fact that one of the scepters was drawn tied to the Warrior Priest's litter in Figure 143 indicates that it was his property. When we consider that the man in Tomb 1 was buried holding one of these scepters, his identification as the Warrior Priest seems certain.

This identification is particularly intriguing because the royal tomb that was looted at Sipán in February of 1987 contained many objects that are nearly identical to those found in Tomb 1. These include circular ear ornaments, a crescent-shaped headdress ornament, gold and silver peanut beads, and a crescent-shaped bell decorated with the Decapitator motif. Moreover, the looted tomb contained a gold and silver scepter (Fig. 153) that is nearly identical to the scepter in Tomb 1. This strongly suggests that the looted tomb also contained a noble who enacted the role of Warrior Priest at the Sacrifice Ceremony. Perhaps Sipán was the designated burial place for priests who participated in this ritual.

When the Sacrifice Ceremony, with its distinct priests and symbolic elements, was first identified in Moche art in 1974, we wondered whether this ceremony was actually enacted by the Moche or whether it was played out by deities in some mythical setting. Since the only evidence of the ceremony was in the artistic depictions, we had no way of knowing whether it was a mythical or real event. The anthropomorphized bird and animal figures certainly seemed mythical, but perhaps these were artistic means to imply the supernatural aspects of real people who were enacting the prescribed roles. Could it be that the Moche actually sacrificed their prisoners of war and consumed their blood? Not until the excavation of Tomb 1 did we have archaeological evidence that this ceremony actually took place, with living individuals enacting the roles of the priests depicted in the art.

Tomb 1 thus provided an extraordinary opportunity to correlate ancient artifacts with those depicted in Moche art. The art enabled us to understand the functional and symbolic purpose of these artifacts, and thereby to identify the status, rank and wealth of the principal individual buried in the tomb, as well as the role that he played in the ceremonial life of his people.

FIG. 154

*Excavation on the
south platform
where Tomb 2
was found.*

VI THE EXCAVATION OF TOMB 2

▼ While the excavation of Tomb 1 was still in progress, we continued to clean and examine other portions of the mud-brick pyramid in an effort to better understand its construction sequence and to search for additional offerings and burials. One afternoon, the archaeologist in charge of a crew working on the south platform reported that he might have found another area of fill similar to that which had led us to Tomb 1 (Fig. 154).

Careful examination confirmed that he had, indeed, located another large area of fill that had been created in ancient times by removing bricks from the solid platform. Like the upper part of Tomb 1, the filled area was nearly square, with its side walls oriented north-south and east-west.

Although Tomb 1 was approximately five meters on each side, the sides of this chamber were only about four meters each.

When the excavators reached a depth of 2.40 meters below ground surface, they found a llama skull buried in the southeast quadrant of the chamber. Then, a few centimeters below the llama skull, and closer to the west side of the chamber, they found the burial of an adult male, extended and lying on his back with his head to the north (Fig. 155). He had been buried in a cane coffin, along with at least fourteen gourd containers, a ceramic dipper, a large copper crown, and a feathered headdress ornament with a large copper shaft.

Like the male burial above Tomb 1, this man's feet were missing. It was determined that they had been cut off at the ankles before the individual was buried (Verano ms.b).

Leaving this burial in position in one half of the filled chamber, we continued to excavate the other half. If this was another tomb like Tomb 1, we would find roof beams somewhere in the next meter of fill. And there they were,

FIG. 155

Burial in upper part of Tomb 2.

seventy-three centimeters below the male burial. They formed a grid of decomposed beams almost identical to the ones that roofed the funerary chamber of Tomb 1. Was it possible that we had actually found a second royal tomb? Because we were on the south platform rather than in the central pyramid, and the dimensions of the chamber were smaller than those of Tomb 1, we postulated that if it was a tomb, it probably contained someone of lesser status, and that the contents would probably be fewer and of lesser quality. Nevertheless, we were excited about the prospect of a second royal tomb and eager to proceed with its excavation.

By March of 1988, the excavation of Tomb 1 was nearly complete. We were clearing the floor of its burial chamber, and recording the position of each of the remaining ceramic vessels before they were removed and transported to the museum. As the final cleaning was completed, we turned our full attention to the south platform hoping that we had indeed found a second tomb, and that it would continue to provide the astounding quantity and quality of information that flowed from our excavation of Tomb 1.

We were not disappointed. We proceeded to remove the disintegrated roof beams and the fill below them. Then, exactly as in Tomb 1, clusters of copper straps began to appear near the center of the chamber. Soon these clusters defined the four corners of what had been a plank coffin. As expected, it was smaller than that of Tomb 1, measuring 1.85 by 0.95 meters (Fig. 156). This plank coffin had been

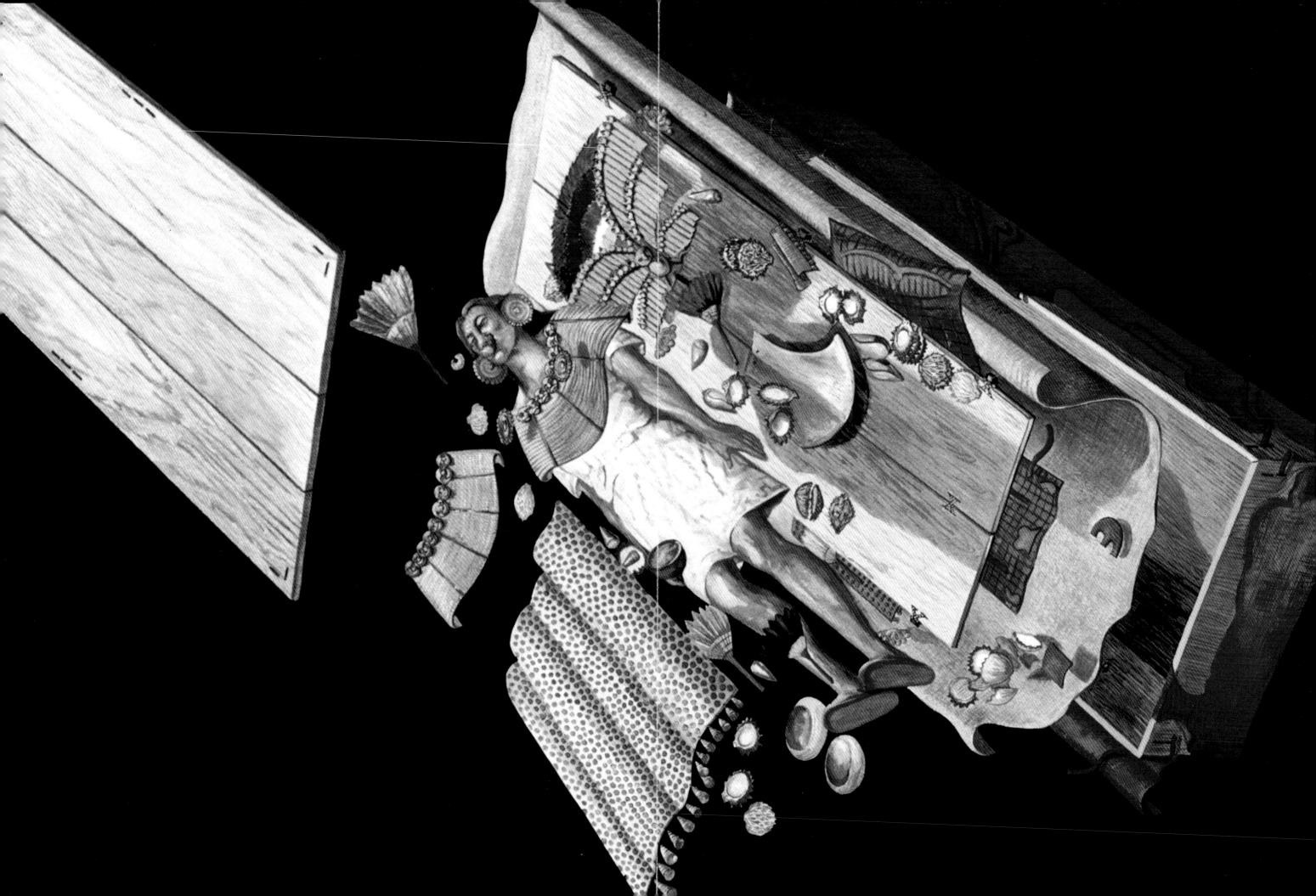

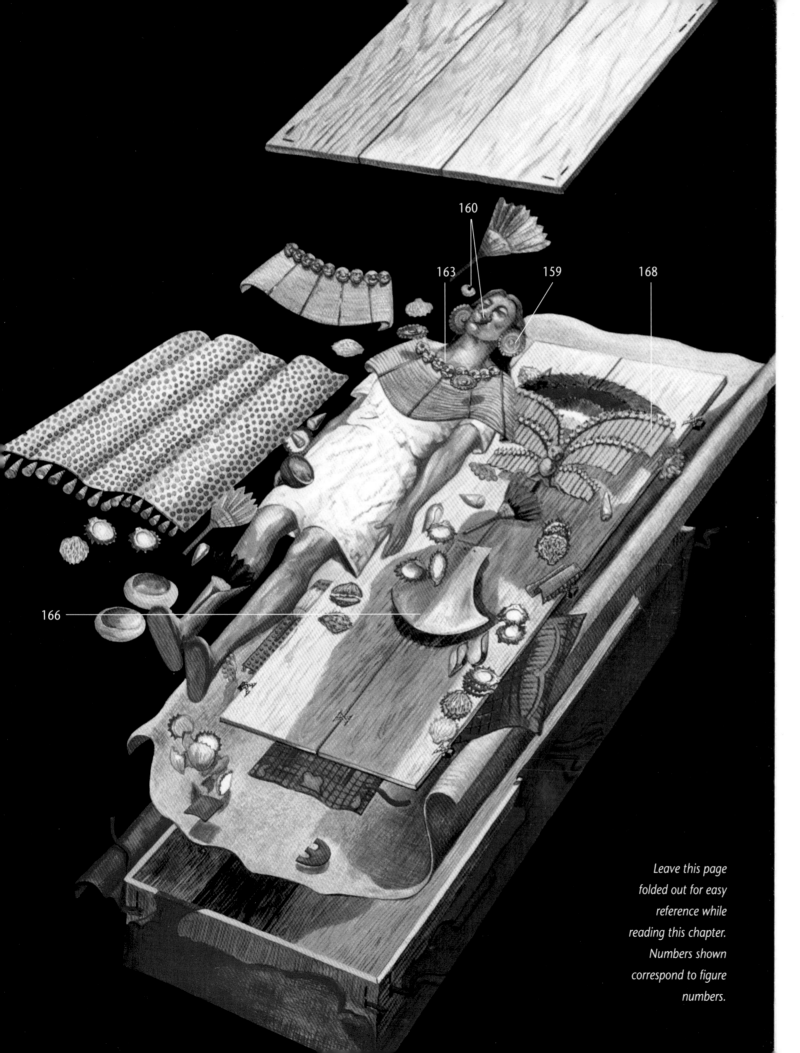

160

163   159   168

166

Leave this page folded out for easy reference while reading this chapter. Numbers shown correspond to figure numbers.

wrapped with a red cloth that had long since decomposed, leaving only a slight trace of its weave and a fine reddish powder.

Now we were certain that we had found another royal tomb. This time we knew what we were excavating, and we could proceed with greater confidence, using the techniques that we had developed in excavating, recording, and removing the Tomb 1 materials. We could plan the best excavation strategies, anticipating how much and what kinds of equipment, labor, and conservation supplies would be needed. This is not to say that we were overly confident. After all, our entire understanding of the nature of Moche royal tombs was based on a sample of one, plus a few insights gained from cleaning and studying the remains of the plundered tomb. Nevertheless, this second tomb was so similar to Tomb 1 that we felt that we could excavate it in a manner that would provide optimum results.

The procedure of first excavating the contents of the central coffin had worked well with Tomb 1, and we used it again. Beneath the residue of three wood planks that formed the lid of the coffin, we found traces of a coarse cotton burial shroud. It had been wrapped around the body of the deceased and around most of the contents of the coffin.

Beneath this shroud were hundreds of small copper discs. Apparently they had been sewn onto a textile, which also had a row of copper cones forming a decorative fringe along its lower edge. Presumably, this was a banner similar to the ones bearing male images in Tomb 1 (Fig. 62). It had been placed over the waist and upper legs of the deceased.

As in Tomb 1, the individual was lying face up in a fully extended position, with the skull at the south end of the coffin. The skull was badly crushed and had splintered into hundreds of pieces by the weight of the soil pressing down as the roof beams and plank coffin decomposed. On each side of the skull were large circular ear ornaments (Fig. 158) that were probably worn by the individual at the time of burial. In the center of each was a human face made of sheet gold, with eyes of turquoise. Each face was surrounded by concentric circles of inlaid turquoise and sheet gold. Encircling these was a gilded copper rim with tiny, projecting spheres (Fig. 159).

An ornate nose ornament, positioned over the lower part of the face, may also have been worn by the deceased at the time of burial. It consisted of an oval disc of sheet metal, half gold and half

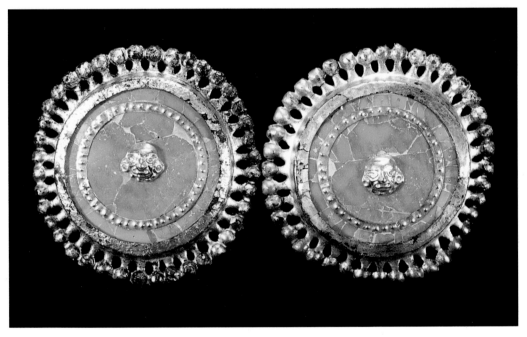

FIG. 158

(top) Ear
ornaments
in situ.

FIG. 159

(bottom) Ear
ornaments
cleaned and
reconstructed.
Dia. 10.5 cms.

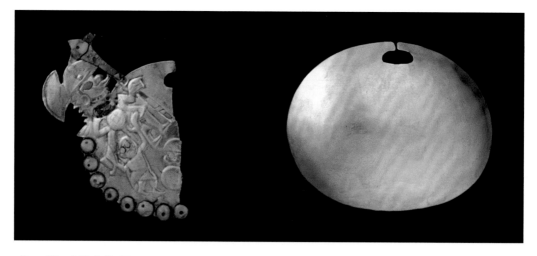

FIG. 160

(top) Half of a gold and silver nose ornament H. 8.5 cms. (left), and a gold nose ornament H. 7.3 cms. (right).

FIG. 161

(bottom) Incised warclubs on the interior (concave) surface of the nose ornament shown in Figure 160 right.

silver (Fig. 160, left). The two halves were joined together by a vertical seam at the center. The silver portion was badly corroded, and only a small fragment of it could be recovered. However, it was apparently a mirror image of the other half, so the original form could be reconstructed. On each half there were two low relief figures: a large, elaborately dressed warrior holding a warclub, and a smaller individual with upraised arms wearing a simple garment. In addition, a human head was depicted near the vertical seam, along with what appears to be a circular shield.[14] The gold half of this nose ornament had a row of round turquoise beads around its lower edge, each set neatly into a circular depression in the sheet metal. At first we assumed that the silver half would have had a similar row of turquoise beads around its lower edge, although that portion of the sheet silver had completely decomposed. Yet no turquoise beads were found in that area. Either the silver half lacked beads, or they were made of a material that has decomposed.

A second nose ornament, made of hammered gold (Fig. 160, right), was found alongside the individual's right cheek. It closely resembled the gold nose ornament from the looted tomb (Fig. 36), as well as the pair of oval nose ornaments from Tomb 1 (Fig. 78). This one, however, had a subtle distinguishing feature — on the inside surface someone had incised two warclubs (Fig. 161). These would have been seen by the wearer holding the nose ornament before putting it on, but were not visible when the ornament was being worn. Were these meant symbolically to ensure that the wearer would never be unarmed?

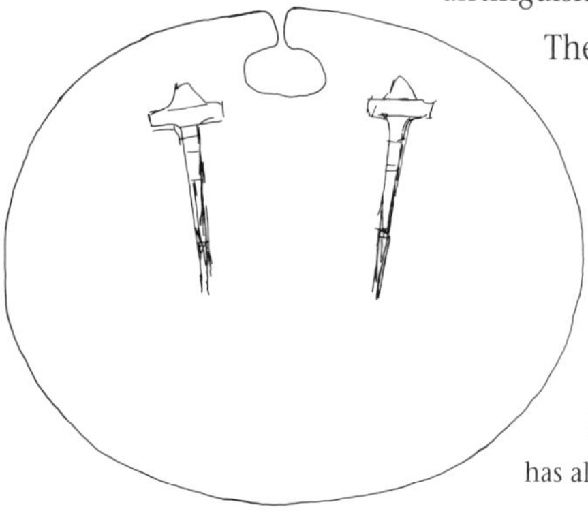

The deceased was wearing two necklaces of human-head beads (Fig. 162). The faces were smiling on one necklace and frowning on the other (Fig. 163). The complementarity of smiling and frowning faces, so superbly

---

[14] A body for this head may have been on the adjacent silver portion of the nose ornament which has almost completely disintegrated.

FIG. 162

*(top) Gilded
copper necklaces of
smiling and frowning
human-head beads
in situ.*

FIG. 163

*(bottom) Gilded
copper necklaces of
smiling and frowning
human-head beads
cleaned and
reconstructed.
Average H. 5.8 cms.*

FIG. 164

Inside the plank coffin, showing skeleton and grave contents.

portrayed on these two necklaces, is heretofore unknown in ancient Peruvian art and remains a mystery.

Immediately beneath the necklaces were thousands of shell beads (Fig. 162) — the remains of two beaded pectorals, similar to those found in Tomb 1. Both consisted exclusively of white beads, strung with the customary four metal spacer bars.

After the pectorals were removed, the individual's skeleton was uncovered and recorded (Fig. 164). Once again, John Verano was able to examine the skeleton *in situ* and after it had been removed to the museum. He concluded that the individual was an adult male, between thirty-five and forty-five years of age at the time of his death. Although he was only about 160 centimeters (five feet two inches) tall, his bones were large and exhibited evidence of strong muscle attachments. There were no signs of ill health or poor nutrition (Verano ms.b).

On the left side of the body were two copper bells (Fig. 165), similar in form to the gilded copper bells in the central coffin of Tomb 1 (Figs. 107, 108, 109). They were almost certainly suspended from long ribbons hanging from an elaborate headdress. Also on the left side of the body was what appeared to have been a miniature banner made of gilded copper platelets that were sewn onto the upper surface of a textile. It had a row of tiny gilded copper cones along the bottom edge.

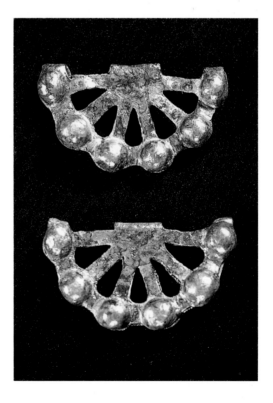

In contrast to the primary individual in Tomb 1, this person was not wearing bracelets. He did, however, wear metal slippers — copper rather than silver — with rounded tops that covered the toes and upper front part of the feet.

Beside his right hand was a copper cup. Near his body were the remains of four feathered headdress ornaments, each with a copper shaft. Two lay over his legs, one lay under his torso, and one was near his head. Also near his head were two circular copper headdress ornaments. Perhaps these three ornaments formed part of a headdress, the perishable portions of which had long since decomposed. Such a headdress may

FIG. 165

Copper bells.
W. 6.3 cms.

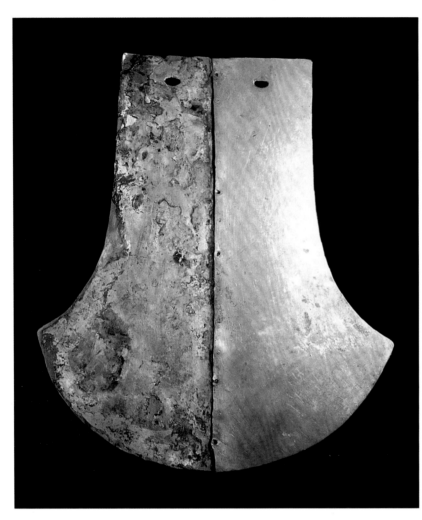

FIG. 166

———

Gold and silver
backflap.
H. 28.6 cms.

have resembled the one found in the upper part
of the coffin of the principal figure in Tomb 1
(see pg. 57).

As in Tomb 1, there were sea shells inside the
individual's coffin. They appeared to have been
wrapped in the shroud, close to the body. Although there were fewer shells than in Tomb 1,
the same two types of shell were present:
Spondylus spp. and *Conus fergusonii.* Near the individual's right ankle were two gourd bowls.

Beneath the body was a large backflap (Fig.
166). It was made from two vertical halves, one
of gold and one of silver, which were edge-welded together along the central axis. Two holes
near the top of the backflap were used to sus-
pend it from a warrior's belt, precisely as shown
in Moche art (Fig. 137).[15]

Under the backflap, we found the remnants
of two wide wood planks tied together with cotton cordage (Fig. 167). They are analogous to
the wood slats beneath the principal figure in
Tomb l, serving to keep the body rigid inside the
burial shroud.

Lying on the wood planks, beneath where
the man's head had rested, was a spectacular
headdress ornament of gilded copper (Figs. 167,
168, 169). At its center were the head and body

———

[15] No backflap of this type had ever been found before,
but similar backflaps are often shown in Moche art with
one half dark and the other half light. Apparently this
dichotomy of hue indicated the two types of metal used.
A fragment of the strap that tied this backflap to a belt
indicates that the strap was made of multiple strands of
cotton yarn, skillfully plaited into a band.

FIG. 167

Inside the
plank coffin,
showing
decomposed
wood frame
and owl
headdress.

FIG. 168

Owl
headdress
in situ.

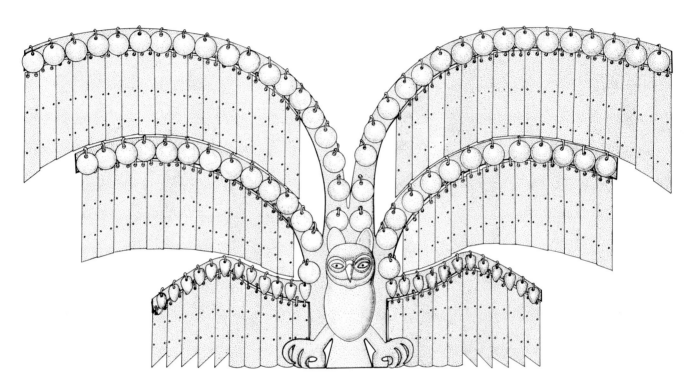

FIG. 169

*Original
form
of owl
headdress.
W. 59.5 cms.*

FIG. 170

*Burial chamber
during excavation
of the burials
placed around
the plank coffin.*

of an owl, shown frontally in nearly three-dimensional sculpture. The owl's eyes were inlaid with white shell and turquoise. Arching outward from each side of the owl were three long metal bands, each covered with bangles suspended from wires. Numerous metal feathers hung from wires that passed through perforations along the lower edge of the bands. Similar headdress ornaments are depicted in Moche art, but since none had previously been excavated we had no idea what they were made of or how they were assembled. We were astounded with the complexity of this object. When worn, it would have been in constant movement as the bangles and feathers swung free. The shimmering appearance of its reflected light must have been dazzling.

When the headdress ornament and the wood planks on which it rested were removed, we were nearing the coffin floor. A few more small objects of copper were found, along with what might

have been another banner. Only a few fragments of gilded copper sheet and some organic
material remained of the latter.

Once the coffin was empty, we were able to
recognize the three planks that formed its floor.
As with the coffin in Tomb 1, the center plank
was not attached to the other planks — again
indicating that the coffin had been assembled in
place, and was subsequently filled with funerary
contents.

FIG. 171

*Original
appearance
of the copper
headdress worn
by the child at
the foot of the
plank coffin.*

With the coffin empty, we then proceeded to excavate the area around it (Fig. 170). As expected,
it was similar to the burial chamber of Tomb 1. The sides and head of the chamber had the same
benches with niches built into them: two niches on each side and one at the head. The side niches
were filled with ceramic and gourd vessels. The niche at the head of the chamber contained the remains of two rectangular boxes, one of wood and the other of copper. The niche also contained a
ceramic stirrup spout bottle in the form of a lizard, analogous to the pair of stirrup spout bottles in
the form of lizards found in the niche at the head of Tomb 1.

To the left of the principal figure, we found a cane coffin containing the body of a male between
fourteen and seventeen years of age (Verano ms.b), lying on his back in a fully extended position
with his head to the north and his arms at his sides (Fig. 170). On his chest were two large copper
discs which may have been part of a headdress.

Lying crosswise at the feet of the principal figure was a smaller cane coffin. It contained the body
of an eight- to ten-year-old child, lying on its back in a fully extended position with its head to the
east and its arms at its sides (Fig. 170). The child was wearing a copper headdress with a human face
in front (Fig. 171). There were at least sixteen gourd bowls inside the coffin, and one ceramic stirrup
spout bottle with an oblate chamber. Also inside the coffin were the skeletons of a dog and a snake.
The dog lay on its right side on top of the child, with its head over the child's pelvis and its tail over
the child's feet. The snake lay extended in the northwest corner of the coffin near the child's feet.
This dog was reminiscent of the dog inside the cane coffin of the adult male buried next to the principal figure in Tomb 1. However, the snake remains an enigma; no other Moche burial
previously excavated contained a snake.

As we continued cleaning the burial chamber floor, we found two other human burials (Fig. 172).

FIG. 172

Burial chamber showing the niches and burials that surrounded the plank coffin.

On the left side of the principal figure, positioned between his plank coffin and the cane coffin containing the adult male, was the burial of a nineteen- to twenty-five-year-old female (*ibid*.). She was not in a coffin, but probably had been wrapped in a burial shroud. She was lying on her back in a fully extended position with her head to the south. Her left arm was at her side; her right arm was slightly bent, with her right hand resting on her abdomen. Over her torso were the fragmentary remains of numerous discs of gilded copper that had presumably been sewn onto a textile.

On this woman's head was a large copper headdress (Fig. 173) that was similar to the one worn by the woman at the foot of the principal figure in Tomb 1 (Figs. 132, 133). It is curious that these headdresses are so similar, and that each is worn by a woman who had been placed in the grave of a noble. Perhaps the headdress was related to a specific female role.

The remaining human burial was that of an eighteen- to twenty-two-year-old female, located on the right side of the principal figure (*ibid*.). In contrast to the other three bodies, which were buried in cane coffins and/or burial shrouds, this individual appears to have had nothing encasing the body. She was lying on her stomach with her right arm at her side. Her left arm extended out from her shoulder, and was bent with the elbow propped against the wall forming one of the side benches. There were no associated grave goods.

At the feet of this woman, in the northeast corner of the burial chamber, was a large adult llama (Fig. 172). It had been decapitated and was lying on its left side with its feet tied together. Its head may be the one found in the fill above the roof beams when this tomb was first being excavated (see pg. 143).

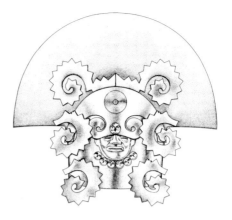

FIG. 173

(top) Original appearance of the copper headdress worn by the woman on the left side of the principal figure.

FIG. 174

(bottom) Burial chamber of Tomb 2 as it might have appeared at the time of the funeral.

Once the burial chamber had been filled with its contents, the roof was constructed, exactly as had been done in Tomb 1. Three short upright posts had been built into the benches along both the east and the west walls. Each row of three posts supported a long horizontal beam on which cross beams were laid parallel to one another, spanning the width of the burial chamber. The area above the tomb was subsequently filled, and in this fill the adult male and llama head had been buried (Fig. 174).

Both Tomb 1 and Tomb 2 were built after the latest phase of pyramid construction was completed (Fig. 40), and probably date to approximately the same time period. They are similar to one

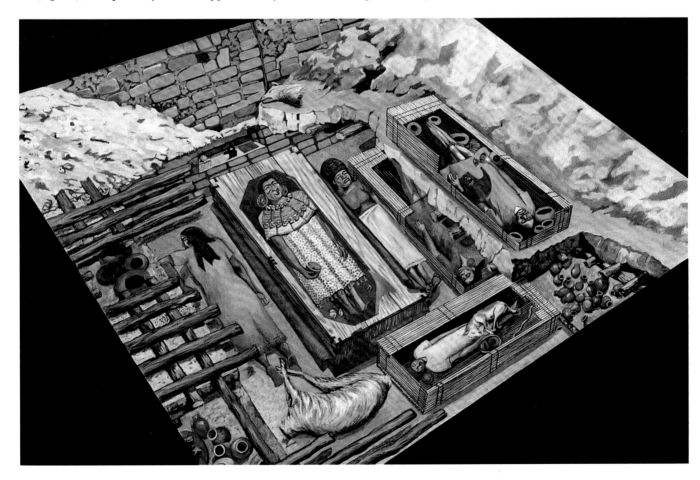

FIG. 175

Offerings found
near Tomb 2.

FIG. 176

Contents of one
of the offerings
near Tomb 2.

another in having a plank coffin for the principal individual, in the overall form and construction
of the burial chamber, in their secondary burials and associated grave contents, and even in the
footless individual buried in the fill above the roof beams. The most significant difference between
the two tombs was one of scale — Tomb 2 was consistently smaller in overall dimensions and had
considerably fewer grave contents. Moreover, the overall quality of grave contents in Tomb 2 was
lower than in Tomb 1. There were fewer gold objects, fewer objects with inlay, and fewer objects
with complex iconography. Whereas Tomb 1 had some matching objects of gold and silver, such as
nose ornaments and backflaps, in Tomb 2 there was a greater propensity to combine gold and silver
in a single object, e.g., the nose ornament (Fig. 160, left) and the backflap (Fig. 166).

These features, combined with the location of Tomb 2 in the south platform rather than in the
central pyramid, imply that it contained a person of lower status than the Warrior Priest in Tomb 1.
But who was he?

The contents of his coffin suggest that he may have been the Bird Priest of the Sacrifice Ceremony.
His large owl headdress and backflap are similar to the owl headdress and backflap frequently worn
by the Bird Priest. Furthermore, he was buried with a copper cup near his right hand. This cup is similar to the upper portion of the tall goblets used in the Sacrifice Ceremony (Figs. 143, 146).

As we identified the individuals in Tomb 1 and Tomb 2 as participants in the Sacrifice Ceremony,
we began to wonder if the actual ceremony took place here as well. The answer was soon revealed to
us approximately ten meters west of Tomb 2. There we found the decomposed remains of numerous
beams that had roofed and sealed small rectangular rooms (Fig. 175). These rooms contained hun-

FIG. 177

Human foot
in an offering
near Tomb 2.

dreds of ceramic vessels, many similar to those found in Offering 1 and Tombs 1 and 2 (Fig. 176). Associated with the ceramic vessels were human and llama bones and miniature ornaments and implements made of sheet copper, mixed with quantities of ash and organic residue. Among the human remains were the articulated bones of human hands and feet (Fig. 177), quite possibly the trophies taken from sacrificed prisoners whose bodies were dismembered, exactly as shown in Moche art (Fig. 144). And among the miniature copper objects were warclubs, shields, headdresses, and goblets (Figs. 178, 179). The latter were the same shape as the goblet used in the Sacrifice Ceremony (compare with Figs. 143, 146). Had we found the offerings of material that resulted from the enactment of the Sacrifice Ceremony? If so, Sipán was not only the burial place for the principal priests who participated in the Sacrifice Ceremony, but also the place where the ceremony was staged.

FIG. 178

(left) Miniature copper warclubs H. 10 cms. and shields in an offering near Tomb 2.

FIG. 179

(right) Miniature copper goblet H. 3 cms. and basin in an offering near Tomb 2.

FIG. 180

Tomb 3,
located
deep inside
the mud-brick
pyramid.

VII THE EXCAVATION OF TOMB 3

▼ As we excavated the offerings on the south platform, a third royal tomb was found. It was more than five meters below the present surface of the pyramid, within the earliest phase of construction (Figs. 40, 180). Since it was sealed beneath the later additions, it had to be considerably earlier than Tombs 1 and 2, which were found in the latest phase of construction.

Unlike Tombs 1 and 2, Tomb 3 did not consist of a deep, room-sized burial chamber with a wood beam roof and niches built into its side walls. Instead, this burial was placed in a simple pit measuring approximately 2.60 meters long and 1.70 meters wide. Thus, the discovery of Tomb 3 did not begin with the identification of a large area of fill. In fact, we did not suspect its presence until we found twenty-six ceramic jars that had been placed along the sides of the principal individual (Fig. 181). These were decorated with white and red paint and modeled faces of humans, animals, and birds.

Instead of being placed in a plank coffin like those in Tombs 1 and 2, the individual had been wrapped in a sedge mat and several textile shrouds. During the subsequent centuries, the mat and textiles had almost completely decomposed, exposing the mass of copper objects inside. These had corroded to form a mound approximately 2.30 meters north-south and 0.80 meters east-west (Fig. 181).

FIG. 181

Upper level of Tomb 3.

THIS PAGE:

FIG. 182
—————
Spider beads
in situ.

OPPOSITE PAGE:

FIG. 183
—————
Exploded
view of the
contents
of Tomb 3.

Above the south end of this mound, we found a spectacular gold necklace of ten large beads (Figs. 181, 182), each a masterpiece of goldworking, depicting a spider with a body in the form of a human head (Fig. 184). The spider's legs were attached to an intricate web that formed the front of the bead. The back of the bead was a dish of sheet gold with an exquisite low relief design (Fig. 185).

The realism and delicacy of these beads was truly remarkable. The spiders' legs and webs were superbly crafted of evenly wrought gold wire (Fig. 186). The sheet gold that formed the body and head of each spider as well as the back of the bead was of even thickness, and masterfully hammered to create the low relief surfaces. Inside each bead were three gold spheres which rattled when the beads were moved. The decision to make these spheres of gold rather than the customary copper was almost certainly dictated by the open wire spider web through which they could be viewed. By using gold instead of copper spheres, the ancient craftsmen created a uniformly aesthetic object.

Because the spider bead necklace was found on top of the objects placed above the royal corpse, it must have been one of the last objects put in position before the tomb was closed. What, then, lay below? This tomb was so different from Tombs 1 and 2 that we had no idea what to expect. Nor

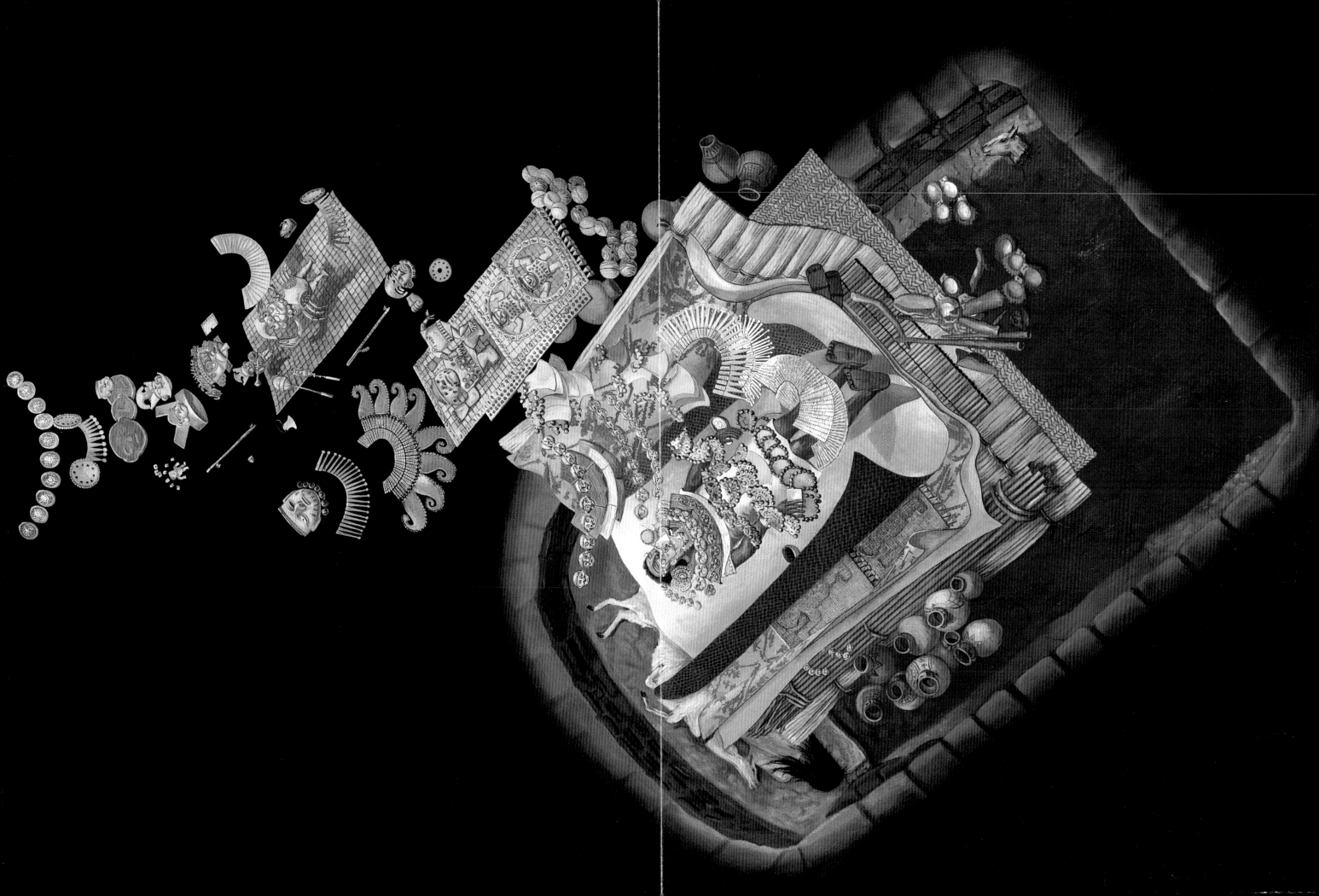

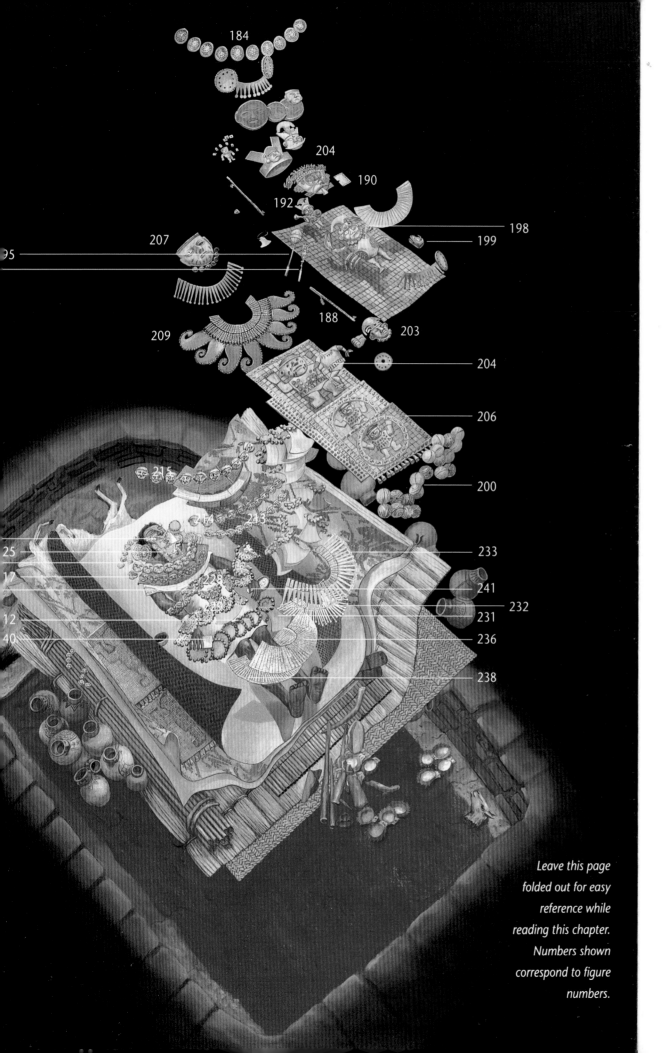

184

204

190

192

198

199

207

95

188

203

209

204

206

200

215

214

243

233

25

17

241

12

232

231

40

236

238

Leave this page folded out for easy reference while reading this chapter. Numbers shown correspond to figure numbers.

FIG. 184
———
Spider beads, cleaned and reconstructed.

FIG. 185

———

(left)
Construction
of the spider
beads.

FIG. 186

———

(above)
Spider bead
cleaned and
reconstructed.
Dia. 8.3 cms.

FIG. 187

*Upper level
of Tomb 3.*

could we enjoy the confidence, as we had when we began excavating Tomb 2, that we could accurately predict the techniques and resources we would need as the excavation proceeded. Nevertheless, we set about recording the tomb with countless photos, detailed scale drawings, and systematic field notes. Because of its earlier date, we named this individual "The Old Lord of Sipán." Little did we know how memorable the next eight months would be as we uncovered the astounding contents of his tomb.

The hundreds of pieces of gilded sheet copper mounded over the body would have appeared like solid gold at the time they were put in the tomb. They had corroded to a pale green color, almost completely obscuring the gold plating. Many of the copper sheets had corroded completely, leaving no metal on their interior, and had subsequently shattered under the pressure of the overlying soil (Fig. 187). This greatly complicated the excavation and identification of the grave contents. Each piece had to be carefully studied *in situ* and its position fully documented if we were ever to reassemble and reconstruct the shattered objects after they were taken from the tomb and moved to the Bruning Museum.

Near the necklace of spider beads were two elaborate discs and a chin strap with triangular elements (see Fig. 34). These suggest that a headdress had been placed in the upper part of the bundle, and that all of its organic portions had long since decomposed. It was similar to the headdress placed near the top of the bundle in Tomb 1 (Figs. 58, 59).

Beneath the headdress were five human faces of sheet metal. One, which was small and made of gilded copper, portrayed a person wearing circular ear ornaments. Three others, made of copper, were round and positioned facing down. The fifth human face, made of gilded copper, wore an elaborate crescent-shaped headdress and a large crescent-shaped nose ornament. The upper level of the tomb also contained a small, standing human figure surrounded by serpent heads, a gilded copper crown with a human head frontlet, and two spear throwers. One of the spear throwers (Fig. 188) had a wood shaft masterfully incised with geometric designs. A copper animal head formed the engaging spur and a copper human head served as the handle. The other spear thrower had a wooden handle carved in the form of a bird head.

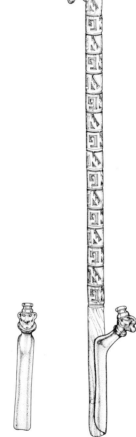

FIG. 188

Spear thrower.
L. 40 cms.

FIG. 189

Gilded copper
feline head
with shell inlay.

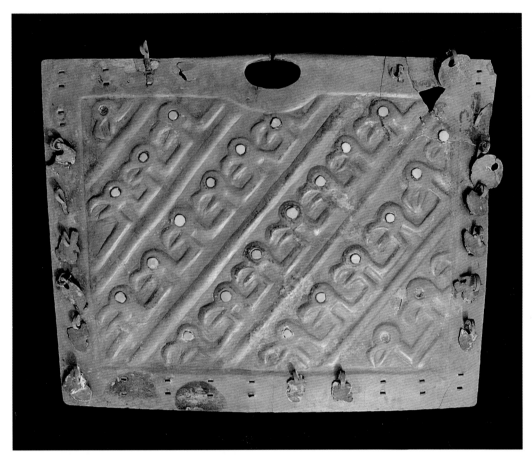

FIG. 190

_____

*Silver and
turquoise nose
ornament.
H. 8.6 cms.*

We then uncovered an extraordinary feline head made of gilded copper (Fig. 189). The ferocious expression of his face was superbly enhanced by shell and stone inlay that provided color to his fangs, teeth, nose, eyes, and ears, and formed a complex double-headed serpent design on his forehead. He wore a double-headed serpent headdress, elaborated with shell inlay and dangling gilded copper discs. This was certainly one of the most remarkable objects of Pre-Columbian metalworking and inlay ever found. But what was it? Originally, it must have been attached to something — perhaps a banner or headdress ornament. We could only speculate about its function, for it was clearly separated from its original context, whatever that may have been.

Along the left side of the feline face was a silver nose ornament (Fig. 190) with a low relief design of repeating birds' heads in diagonal rows and a border decorated with silver discs suspended from wires. The birds' eyes were inlaid with turquoise.

FIG. 191

Drawing Tomb 3
after removal of
the feline head.

Removal of the feline face and silver nose ornament (Fig. 191) revealed a standing warrior made of gilded copper (Fig. 192). Originally, he was probably sewn to a textile to form a banner. The warrior holds a warclub diagonally across his chest and wears an elaborate headdress with a chin strap consisting of triangular elements. On his left wrist is a circular shield, with a circle and checkerboard pattern lightly incised in its polished surface — virtually identical to the enigmatic disc of gold from the looted tomb (Fig. 37). Apparently the looted tomb had a similar warrior. How sad that only his shield remains.

FIG. 192

Gilded
copper
warrior.
H. 27.4 cms.

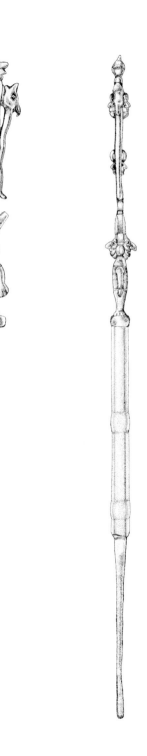

FIG. 193
————
(right)
Original
appearance
of the silver
scepter.
H. 24.3 cms.

FIG. 194
————
(left) Detail
of the silver
scepter finial.

Along the right side of the standing warrior were two scepters — one silver and the other gold. The silver one had an elaborate finial depicting a warrior with a tall rack above his head (Figs. 193, 194). Suspended from the rack was a pair of human heads, while along its sides and top were serpents.

The gold scepter had a rattle at its upper end (Fig. 195). The rattle chamber was almost spherical, with a slightly pointed top, vertical lobes, and a raised horizontal band around its equator. A small loop was attached to the upper part of the handle.[16]

We then found an anthropomorphized crab of gilded copper, facing forward with claws raised (Fig. 196). He wore a necklace of owl-head beads, similar to those from the looted tomb (Fig. 44), and a crescent-shaped headdress with an owl in the center. Shell and stone inlay handsomely accentuated his eyes and crab features (Fig. 197). The figure may have been complete when placed in the tomb, but subsequent corrosion and shattering of the gilded copper has left it in a very delicate and fragmented condition. A painting illustrates its original appearance (Fig. 198).

---

[16] This scepter is remarkably similar to one excavated in a late Moche tomb at Pacatnamu (Ubbelohde-Doering 1983:Abb 59).

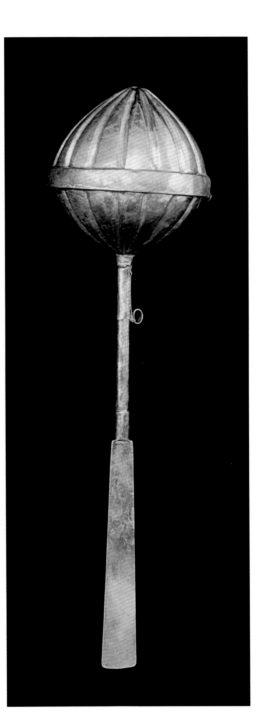

FIG. 195

Gold scepter.
H. 22.6 cms.

FIG. 196

Anthropomorphized crab in situ.

FIG. 197

_(left)
Anthropomorphized
crab. H. 62 cms._

FIG. 198

_(right) Original
appearance of the
anthropomorphized
crab._

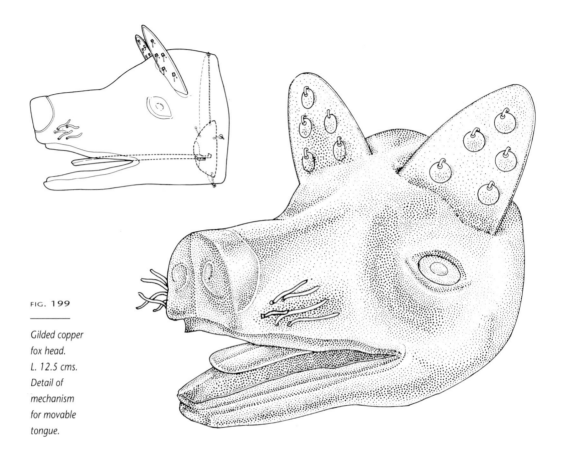

FIG. 199

*Gilded copper
fox head.
L. 12.5 cms.
Detail of
mechanism
for movable
tongue.*

To the left of the crab was a fox head (Fig. 199) which was probably part of a headdress. Its large ears and open mouth were ornamented with discs suspended from wires, and its eyes were inlaid with shell and stone. Originally, its tongue was suspended in such a way that it moved from side to side in its open mouth. Near the fox head was another pair of elaborate discs and a chin strap with triangular elements, suggesting that another headdress had been placed in this part of the tomb.

When these objects were removed, we found the remains of a large rectangular textile that had been covered with platelets of gilded copper. Beneath the textile was another set of remarkable objects. Near the foot of the burial, there were twenty large spherical bells of gilded copper (Fig. 200, 202). They are similar to the tiny sphere from the looted tomb (Fig. 37), but these are approximately nine centimeters in diameter. Similar objects are shown in Moche art tied to staffs to create rattles (Fig. 201).

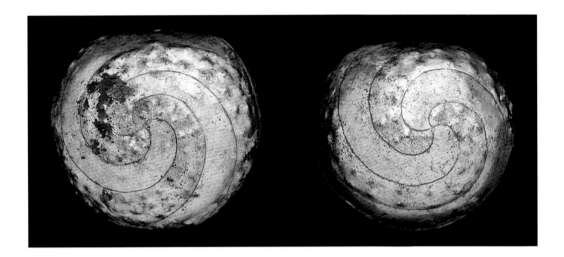

Over the central part of the burial was a human face mask, about half life-sized, wearing a large crescent headdress, circular ear ornaments with suspended bangles, and a necklace of owl-head beads (Figs. 202, 203). It was made of silver and originally had eyes of inlaid shell. Curiously, the inlay in the left eye was missing and was not found elsewhere in the tomb; it has a one-eyed appearance just as it did when it was placed there. To the right of this mask was a gilded copper hand, lying palm upright with the fingers closed. Again, we were puzzled by the fact that both the face mask and the hand appeared to be merely parts of larger objects. We searched in vain for the other parts, and when they were not found we began to suspect that some of the objects had been deliberately disassembled before placement in the tomb.

Our suspicions were confirmed with the next level uncovered. To our amazement, positioned over the central part of the tomb was the body that had originally been attached to the spectacular

FIG. 200
—————
(top) Spherical
bells. Dia. 9 cms.

FIG. 201
—————
(bottom) Moche
fineline drawing
depicting spherical
bells tied to staffs.

FIG. 202

*Removal of
silver mask.
Spherical bells
can be seen in
the foreground.*

FIG. 203

Silver mask.
H. 23.3 cms.
without
necklace.

FIG. 204

Anthropomorphized
feline cleaned and
reconstructed.
H. 56.5 cms.

feline head we had found earlier (Fig. 189). When the head and body were combined, this extraordinary creature stood approximately sixty centimeters high (Fig. 204). He wore a necklace of owl-head beads, and his legs and arms were spread in a threatening posture. His copper claws were fully exposed, projecting menacingly from his hands and feet and giving him an aura of awesome power. Nothing like this was known to have been made in ancient Peru. Surely it must have been a well known and highly revered object to the Moche. Therefore, its placement in the tomb — disassembled with its parts separated — is all the more enigmatic. The right arm was actually found in the southwest corner of the burial — almost a meter from the rest of the body. Moreover, the left leg was missing altogether.[17] The reason for the mutilation is not clear, and seems particularly odd, since neither of the other two royal tombs contained anything that appeared to have been disassembled.

Beneath the feline body were three banners, similar to those found in Tomb 1 (Fig. 62). Each had a single figure facing forward with arms raised and feet splayed (Figs. 205, 206). Their bodies were elaborated with numerous gilded copper discs and triangles suspended by wires from the torso and face. They wore large circular ear ornaments and visors. Surrounding their bodies were rectangular gilded copper platelets.

On one of the banners, the human figure was large, and an *ulluchu* was embossed on each of the platelets along the banner's outer edge. To our amazement, when we lifted these platelets, there was an actual *ulluchu* beneath each. When sewing these platelets to the background fabric, the Moche had placed a real fruit under the hollow of each embossed one. Hidden from view in their special casings, they probably gave the banner greater sanctity.

The figures on the other two banners were smaller. Although each was surrounded by a band of sheet metal embossed with *ulluchus* (Fig. 206), no actual fruits were found under these bands.

Peering out from a mass of copper objects above the banners was a life-sized burial mask that originally had been placed over the face of the deceased (Fig. 205). It had a crescent nose ornament, and a necklace of owl-head beads (Fig. 207). Like the silver mask that had been found above (Fig. 203), the shell inlay from the left eye was missing at the time it was placed in the tomb.

Below the lower edge of the burial mask was a series of triangular sheets of gilded copper with a gilded copper disc suspended from the lower point of each (Fig. 205). These probably formed an elaborate chin strap for another headdress.

When we removed the triangles, the face mask, and the banner bearing the largest human figure,

---

[17] The cleaning and reconstruction of this object as shown in Figure 204 was done at the Bruning Museum. The left leg was fabricated at that time in order to provide a better sense of the original object.

FIG. 205

*Banners and
burial mask
in situ.*

FIG. 206

(left) Banner
cleaned and
partially
reconstructed.
Dia. 34 cms.

FIG. 207

(right)
Burial mask.
H. 23 cms.
without
necklace.

FIG. 208

Octopus
pectoral
in situ.

FIG. 209

*Original
appearance
of the octopus
pectoral.
W. 90 cms.*

we exposed an enormous metal pectoral (Fig. 208). This pectoral, ninety centimeters across, would have completely covered the chest and shoulders of the wearer, its large curved tentacles visually transforming him into an anthropomorphized octopus![18] The pectoral consists of nearly 100 separate parts, each carefully crafted of multiple metal sheets that had been delicately soldered together. The painting in Figure 209 attempts to capture its original beauty, the complexity of its construction, and the remarkable combination of materials that enhance its dramatic presence.

When we removed these items and the other two banners, we found another rectangular textile covered with gilded copper platelets. In contrast to the one above, however, the platelets were round rather than rectangular, and the textile they were sewn to was much finer, with a more open weave.

When it was removed, numerous other items became visible along the entire length of the burial. We could see that we were nearing the body of the deceased, and as we did so the quantity and quality of objects was increasing. In the central part of the burial were ten gilded copper discs, each

---

[18] This pectoral and the banner with the anthropomorphized crab are the first objects found at Sipán that depict maritime themes. All the other iconography focuses on militarism and prisoner sacrifice. It may be that the crab and octopus were seen by the Moche as maritime counterparts to the spider because of their appearance. Alternatively, they may have been included because of their propensity to capture their opponents.

nine centimeters in diameter, with a series of hollow spheres around its circumference (Figs. 210, 212). The hollow spheres contained copper pellets which made them rattle when moved. It is not clear how these bells were used.

On each side of the burial was a copper bowl standing upright and filled with unknown substances, black in the right bowl and white in the left (Fig. 187).

Near the neck of the individual lay multiple sets of necklaces, ear ornaments, and nose orna-

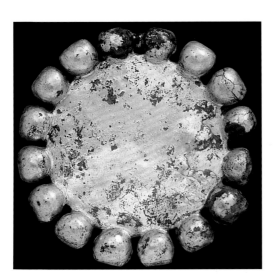

ments of gold and silver, piled one on top of another in a dazzling display of wealth and opulence (Fig. 211). There were six necklaces, each consisting of ten beads.[19] All originally had eyes inlaid with shell. Three of the necklaces were silver — one consisting of deity-head beads with shell teeth (Fig. 213), one of human-head beads without teeth (Fig. 214), and one of deity-head beads with both shell teeth and large shell fangs (Fig. 215).

[19] It is remarkable that nearly all of the necklaces at Sipán consist of ten beads. This suggests that ten may have been an important number to the Moche.

OPPOSITE PAGE:

FIG. 210
—————
Excavation nearing the body of the principal individual.

THIS PAGE:

FIG. 211
—————
(top) Jewelry near the individual's head.

FIG. 212
—————
(bottom) Gilded copper disc cleaned. Dia. 9 cms.

FIG. 213

———

(top) Silver
deity-head
bead with
shell inlay.
H. 5.7 cms.

FIG. 214

———

(bottom) Silver
human-head
bead in situ.
H. 7.9 cms.

FIG. 215

*Fragment of a
silver deity-head
bead with
shell inlay.
H. 7.9 cms.*

FIG. 216

*Gold human-head
bead* in situ.

THE EXCAVATION OF TOMB 3 ▼

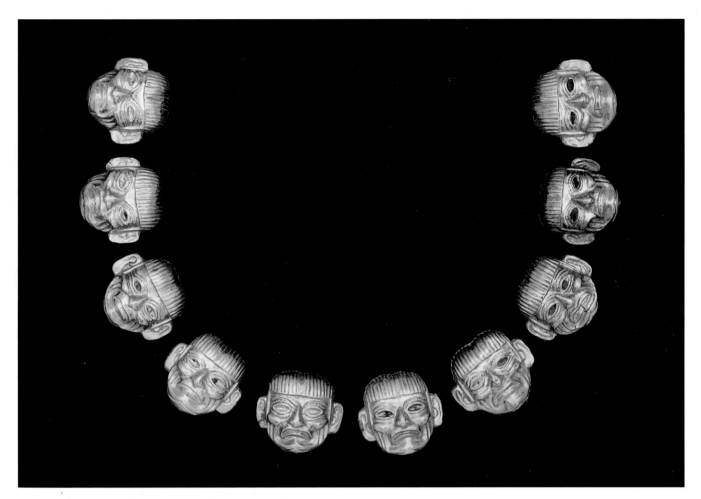

Two of the necklaces were gold, one with human heads of an old man with a wrinkled face (Figs. 216, 217) and the other with feline heads that had red shell teeth and fangs (Fig. 218). The latter beads, 6.3 centimeters in diameter, are miniature versions of the feline-head beads from the looted tomb (Figs. 24, 25), which are sixteen centimeters in diameter. The final necklace, of gilded copper, was of simple human-head beads.

Scattered among the necklaces was an impressive assortment of nose ornaments. By far the most extraordinary of these depicted a standing warrior figure. He was nestled down inside a cluster of gold, silver, and shell jewelry. We first noticed his gold warclub held in his tiny gold fist. Delicately excavating with a fine brush and spoon, we revealed his gold feet, turquoise tunic, and crescent-

FIG. 217

*Gold human-head
beads cleaned.
H. 5.3 cms. each.*

199

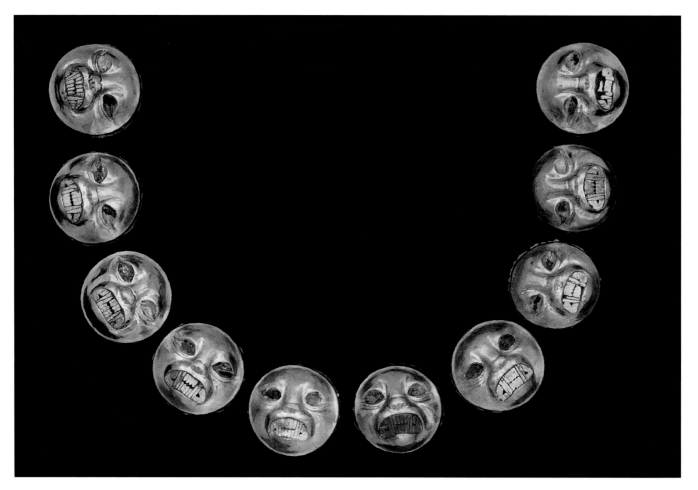

FIG. 218

*Gold
feline-head
beads with
shell inlay
cleaned.
Dia. 6.3 cms.
each.*

shaped gold nose ornament. His face and headdress were underneath a pectoral made of hundreds of shell beads. It was only after the removal of this pectoral that the full warrior was revealed. Catching the sun for the first time in nearly 2,000 years, he peered up at us through inlaid eyes, wearing a magnificent owl headdress with long arching wings from which delicate gold feathers were suspended on gold wires (Fig. 219). His body and posture were remarkably similar to the warriors on the ear ornaments in Tomb 1 (Fig. 87). His headdress, however, resembled the full-sized owl headdress found in Tomb 2 (Fig. 169).

His warclub, so prominently held in his right fist, could be removed and replaced at will. The crescent-shaped nose ornament swung freely in the septum of his nose. He stood proudly on a small silver pedestal projecting from the large, square, silver sheet that would have been suspended from

FIG. 219

Warrior nose
ornament
in situ.
H. 11 cms.

the septum of the wearer's nose. The upper wings of the owl headdress — their dangling feathers and discs shimmering with reflected light — would have extended up beneath the wearer's eyes. Every part of this remarkable figure was executed with delicacy and skill. It was a spectacular find — certainly one of the most beautiful nose ornaments ever created.

Near this nose ornament were numerous others. The largest was a gold crescent (Fig. 220). Two others were rectangular: one was plain and made of gold (Fig. 221), and the other was half gold and half silver, with the two halves joined on a diagonal seam across the center.

Three other nose ornaments were oval and made of both silver and gold (Figs. 222, 223, 224). One of these (Fig. 224) depicts a ray combined with birds' heads; the eyes are inlaid with turquoise.

THIS PAGE:

FIG. 220
—————
*Jewelry
near the
individual's
head.*

OPPOSITE PAGE:

FIG. 221
—————
*(top left)
Gold nose
ornament.
H. 4.3 cms.*

FIG. 222
—————
*(top right)
Gold and
silver nose
ornament.
H. 4 cms.*

FIG. 223
—————
*(bottom left)
Gold and
silver nose
ornament.
H. 4.8 cms.*

FIG. 224
—————
*(bottom right)
Gold, silver,
and turquoise
nose ornament.
H. 3.1 cms.*

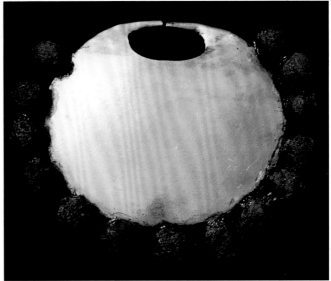

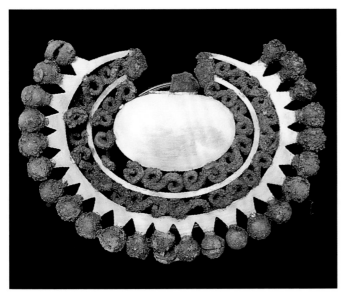

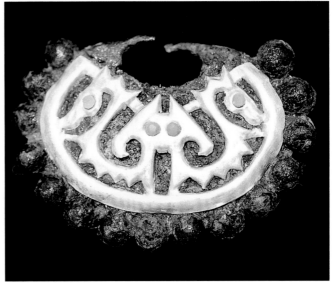

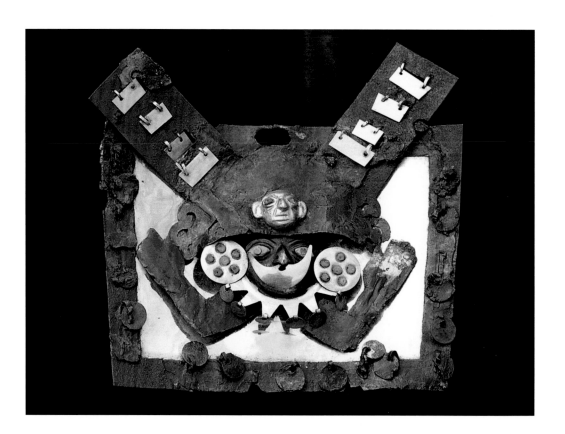

FIG. 225

(top) Gold, silver, and turquoise nose ornament with human head and upraised arms. H. 9 cms.

FIG. 226

(bottom) Gold ear ornaments in situ. Dia. 10.9 cms. each.

Another spectacular nose ornament features the head and upraised arms of a person wearing circular ear ornaments, a crescent-shaped nose ornament, and a headdress with a human head in its center (Fig. 225). It combines silver and gold parts. Inlaid turquoise highlights the eyes and ear ornaments.

There were also two pairs of ear ornaments (Fig. 220), one of gold (Fig. 226) and the other of silver. The small dangling discs covering their faces would have glittered brilliantly in sunlight. They are remarkably similar to the ear ornaments from the looted tomb (Fig. 33) and indicate that the looted tomb also contained one gold pair and one silver pair.

Cleaning the area near the torso and legs of the burial revealed more extraordinary objects (Fig. 227). Over the torso were three beaded pectorals, placed in the same manner as the beaded pectorals in Tomb 1 (Figs. 70-74). Unfortunately, in this tomb the pectorals had broken apart. Their copper spacer bars lay oxidized and scattered, mute testimony to the thousands of intricately ordered beads that had fallen away as the fine cotton strings decomposed centuries ago. Since the beads from distinct pectorals mixed together as they cascaded down over the objects beneath them, it was impossible to reconstruct their original form.

Above the pelvis of the deceased were sets of bells and backflaps like those found in Tomb 1 (Figs. 121, 122, 123), depicting the Decapitator holding a human head in one hand and a knife in the other. But this tomb contained many more of these ornaments — ten gold and ten silver bells (Figs. 228, 229) along with one gold backflap with the Decapitator at the top (Fig. 230). There were also twenty other backflaps that did not depict the Decapitator. Ten of these were gilded copper, with a pair of lizards depicted in the upper part. The other ten, made of silver, were not decorated (Fig. 231).

FIG. 227

Objects near the individual's body.

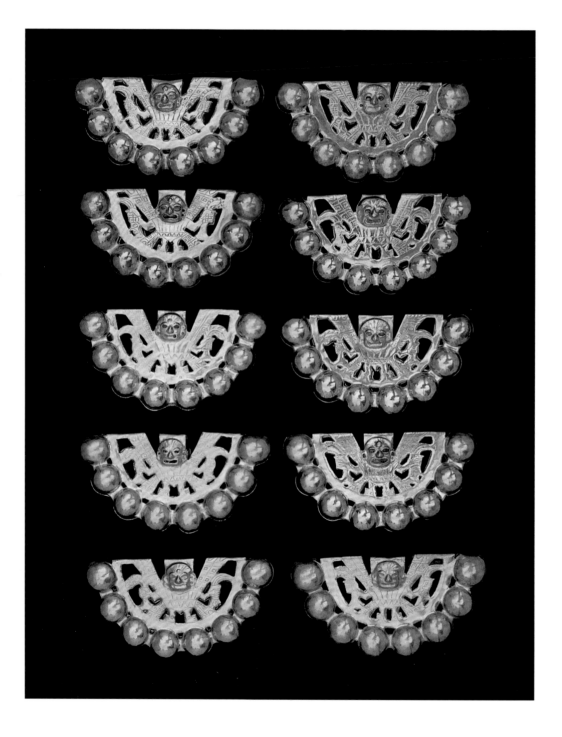

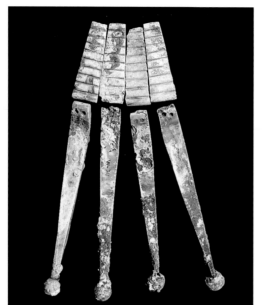

FIG. 232
_____

(left) Portion
of a shell
pectoral.
H. 17.7 cms.

FIG. 233
_____

(right) Portion
of a shell
pectoral.
H. 16.2 cms.

Over the legs of the individual was a mass of intricately crafted shell beads that had been strung into complex pectorals (Fig. 227). Finding them *in situ* made it possible to study their construction and to learn how Moche jewelers combined beads of different sizes and shapes to form impressive ornaments. One pectoral combined short trapezoidal beads and long triangular ones which have spheres at their pointed ends (Fig. 232). Both bead types were familiar to us, because similar gold beads had been recovered from the looted tomb (Figs. 29, 31). Since the looters had torn them from their original context, however, we had no idea that they belonged together. When we saw the shell counterparts in their proper alignment, it was clear they were meant to complement one another — the short, closely-spaced trapezoidal beads supporting the long triangular beads below.

A second pectoral, of similar construction, combined short trapezoidal beads with long triangular beads ending in stylized fish or serpent heads (Fig. 233). Each head was made of spondylus shell and had inlaid turquoise eyes. In the same area we found a pectoral of rectangular shell beads (Fig. 234), each perforated with two long holes (Fig. 236).

Beneath these pectorals was yet another, even more spectacular than those above (Fig. 235). It was made of sixty-one long shell beads, each inlaid with multiple pieces of red shell that cleverly set off an undulating creature, possibly a catfish (Figs. 237, 238). Drilled through their widths, these long beads had been strung adjacent to one another to create a nearly complete circle.

The four shell pectorals had been placed one on top of the other over the lower legs of the deceased in a manner similar to the beaded pectorals found over the lower legs and feet of the Warrior Priest in Tomb 1.

FIG. 234

Shell pectorals
in situ.

FIG. 235

*Shell pectoral
on individual's
lower legs.*

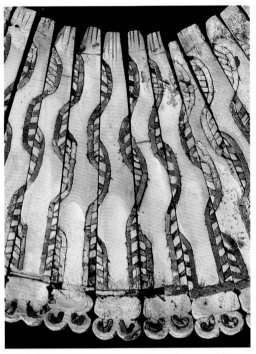

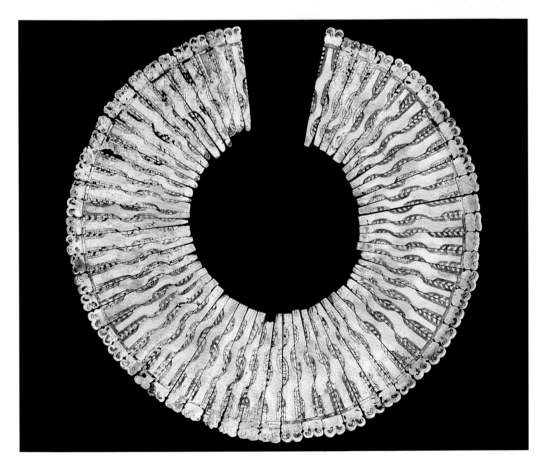

FIG. 236
———
(top left)
Portion of a
shell pectoral.

FIG. 237
———
(top right)
Detail of shell
pectoral cleaned
and reconstructed.
H. 13.2 cms.

FIG. 238
———
(bottom) Shell
pectoral cleaned
and reconstructed.
Dia. 47.5 cms.

FIG. 239

Upper part of
the individual's
skeleton.

FIG. 240

(left) The individual's right hand holding a silver nose ornament.

FIG. 241

(right) Beaded bracelet on individual's left wrist. Note silver ingot in left hand.

Finally, we arrived at the actual body. As we cleared the area of the upper body, we found that the deceased was wearing colorful bracelets consisting of tiny gold, shell, turquoise, and lapis lazuli beads strung in parallel rows and positioned with gold spacer bars (Figs. 239, 241). The gold beads were minute hollow cylinders, identical in form and size to those recovered from the looted tomb (Fig. 28). His right hand held a rectangular silver nose ornament (Fig. 240), and his left hand held a silver ingot (Fig. 241).

The skull was badly broken by the compression of the soil above the tomb, but other parts of the skeleton were better preserved (Figs. 239, 242). The skeletal remains were of an adult male between forty-five and fifty-five years of age. He was about 162 centimeters (five feet three inches) tall. His teeth were heavily worn, with only a ring of enamel remaining on several molars. All of his teeth were present, however, and there were no signs of cavities (Verano ms.b). A large gold ingot had been placed in his mouth, another at the left side of his head, and a third under his head. Two large silver ingots were placed on top of his chin.

THE EXCAVATION OF TOMB 3

FIG. 242

*Removing the
individual's
skeleton.*

Bunched alongside his lower left leg were fragments of eight textiles, three with elaborate tapestry weave designs (Figs. 243, 244). Only small portions of each had survived, but they provide ample evidence that the tomb contents originally included a spectacular array of sumptuous weavings, some of which depicted elaborate mythical scenes.

The body, along with the majority of grave contents, was wrapped in at least three large burial shrouds. Placed between two of these were remnants of two banners, similar to those above the body depicting human figures (Figs. 205, 206). These banners, however, were facing down rather than up, like the banners under the principal individual in Tomb 1.

Beneath the wrapped bundle was a stiff frame that was meant to keep the body rigid. Although we could not determine whether it was made of wood or cane, it clearly was similar to the frames placed beneath the principal figures in Tombs 1 and 2. The bundle and frame were then wrapped in a twined sedge mat. Inside this mat wrapping along the east side of the tomb were twelve long wood lances, sheathed in gilded copper (Fig. 235). Their wood cores were intact when they were

214

placed in the tomb, but their points had been removed. Five of the points had been bent into rings that tied the spear shafts into a bundle. A necklace of gilded copper beads in the form of human heads had been placed over the upper end of the lance bundle.

There was no evidence of either a wood or cane coffin. The sedge mat had apparently been placed on a reed mat that lay on the burial chamber floor. The floor had been covered with a thin coating of red mineral pigment.

At the foot of the tomb was a mound of copper sheathing that had once encased a shield, lances, and a warclub (Fig. 187). Their wood cores had been removed and the sheathing had subsequently been bent, twisted, and broken prior to its placement in the tomb. In this area there was also a small human face of copper. Eight spondylus shells and the skull of a llama were found at the foot of the burial near the northwest corner of the burial chamber.

Carefully cleaning the area around the head of the primary burial, we found the body of a young female (Fig. 242). She was face down with her left arm extended at her side and her right arm splayed out from her body and slightly flexed. She was between sixteen and eighteen years old when she died (Verano ms.b). A llama skeleton lay on top of her right forearm, pelvis, and leg. Its neck was bent back in an unnatural position — perhaps in order to cut its throat in a ritual sacrifice. Both the young woman and the llama were separated from the principal burial by a row of mud bricks that had been placed on the floor of the tomb chamber. They had no associated grave goods. The red pigment that covered the floor beneath the principal burial was not found beneath the woman and llama.

As the excavation of Tomb 3 was being completed, we were left with various questions about the identity of its principal occupant and what relationship he may have had to those buried in Tombs 1 and 2. The remarkable quantity and quality of objects in Tomb 3 clearly demonstrate that this was a person of extremely high status in Moche society. Why, then, did he not have a large, elaborate burial chamber like Tombs 1 and 2, with multiple individuals and hundreds of ceramic vessels? Perhaps this reflects an evolution in Moche funerary practice — large chamber tombs may not have been used until some time later, around A.D. 250 when Tombs 1 and 2 were constructed.

On the basis of tomb contents, it is not possible to identify the principal figure in Tomb 3 as one of the participants in the Sacrifice Ceremony. There were some objects that were nearly identical to those found in Tomb 1 — the tomb of a Warrior Priest — including the crescent-shaped nose ornaments, beaded pectorals, and backflaps and crescent-shaped bells depicting the Decapitator. But Tomb 3 did not have the crescent-shaped headdress ornament that is a characteristic feature of the

FIG. 243

Elaborate
textile
in situ.

FIG. 244

*Elaborate
textile
in situ.*

Warrior Priest in all artistic depictions of him. Nor did his scepter have the trapezoidal box-like chamber that we associate with the Warrior Priest.

Here again, however, the differences may be due to changes in Moche culture during the two centuries intervening between Tombs 3 and 1. We must keep in mind that none of the iconographic depictions of the Sacrifice Ceremony known today is earlier than A.D. 300. It may be that the characteristic features of the Warrior Priest's attire, *as we are accustomed to seeing them*, had not been developed by that time. Perhaps Tomb 3 does contain a Warrior Priest who participated in an early version of the Sacrifice Ceremony, but neither the crescent-shaped headdress ornament nor the scepter with trapezoidal chamber that would become characteristic of the Warrior Priest had yet become part of his ritual paraphernalia.

More data will be needed to resolve these issues. It is wonderful, however, to be able to formulate the questions and develop possible hypotheses that can be tested as new information becomes available. The continuing excavations at Sipán may well provide the information we need. Perhaps someday we will know the identification of the man who was buried in such splendor in Tomb 3 and be able to understand and appreciate his role in Moche society.

FIG. 245

Mannequin
dressed in
replicas of
objects from
Tomb 1.

A GREATER UNDERSTANDING OF MOCHE CIVILIZATION

▼ It will be years before the entire contents of the three royal tombs at Sipán are cleaned, reconstructed, and fully analyzed. Nevertheless, the tombs have already provided a wealth of information which has fundamentally altered our perception of Moche civilization.

MOCHE ROYALTY

Certainly one of the most important insights gained from the Sipán tombs is that the pinnacle of Moche society soared much higher than we had imagined. No Moche burials previously excavated were as large and complex as Tombs 1 and 2, with their room-sized burial chambers containing multiple individuals in separate coffins, surrounded by hundreds of ceramic vessels. Nor had any Moche tombs contained anywhere near the quantity and quality of jewelry and ornaments that were found in the three royal tombs at Sipán.

In the early 1960s, grave robbers looted a massive number of Moche metal objects from the site of Loma Negra, located in the Piura Valley on the northern margin of the Moche kingdom (Fig. 1). Made of gold, silver, and copper, the Loma Negra material included many objects that were remarkably similar in size, form, and even iconography to some of those from Sipán. However, since no archaeological record was made of the Loma Negra finds, we had no documentation of their original context. Because no Moche tombs had previously been excavated with such vast quantities of metal objects, it seemed unlikely that they came from tombs. Instead, we thought that they may have come from a large cache of ritual objects, perhaps from a temple or shrine that had been used by the Moche on ceremonial occasions.

Now, with what we have learned from Sipán, it is almost certain that the Loma Negra treasures *were* from tombs and that Loma Negra was a second location where at least one high status individual was buried with all of his ornaments and ritual paraphernalia. The radiocarbon dates for the Loma Negra treasures are approximately A.D. 300 — essentially contemporary with Tombs 1 and 2 at Sipán.

In 1988, another royal tomb was looted by grave robbers at La Mina, a site in the lower part of the Jequetepeque Valley approximately seventy kilometers south of Sipán (Fig. 1). The tomb was at the foot of a conical hill overlooking the valley floor. It was almost completely destroyed before we were able to locate it, but every effort was made to record all that remained of its original form and contents. Dug partly into bedrock, its burial chamber measured about three meters north-south by two meters east-west. The large mud-brick side walls had been plastered with clay and then painted with colorful geometric designs. The tomb chamber had been roofed about two meters above its clay floor and then sealed with tons of gravel and rock.

We searched the surrounding area for traces of other tombs, but we found none. Yet as the material looted from this tomb began to appear on the art market, it became clear that it was every bit as rich as the royal tombs at Sipán and Loma Negra, and had contained many objects of nearly identical size, form, and iconography. We suspect that it may also date to approximately A.D. 300, a time that must have been something of a golden era on the north coast of Peru.

The royal tombs at Sipán, Loma Negra, and La Mina confirm that in Moche society tremendous wealth was concentrated in the hands of a few individuals, who lived in opulence and were surrounded by lesser nobility. Every valley may have had one or more royal courts, each having little direct contact with the common people, yet connected to one another like the royalty of Europe. Just as European royalty shared a concept of what constituted the trappings of wealth and power, such as crowns, scepters, thrones, and royal carriages, Moche royalty shared insignia of power and status — gold and silver headdresses, nose ornaments, ear ornaments, bracelets, pectorals, necklaces, bells, and scepters. But unlike European royalty, who passed on their jewelry, ornaments, and ritual paraphernalia to successive generations of kings and queens, the Moche took their treasures to the grave. Thus, the immense wealth of ornaments and opulent clothing that garbed these rulers was removed from society and had to be replaced by artisans creating new royal attire for the next lord.

The continuing demand for luxury goods must have ensured the employment of large crews of skilled artisans, who were commissioned by the elite to produce the quantities of luxury objects required to dress successive generations of Moche nobility. This would have nurtured the blossoming of arts and technology that characterizes Moche society.

THE GOLD ENSEMBLE

It is customary for us to view and appreciate the remarkable quality of Moche ornaments and ritual paraphernalia as individual works of art, either in museum collections or in books. We must keep in mind, however, that each was meant to be part of an ensemble consisting of multiple objects. When worn and used together, they would have imparted a grandeur and elegance far greater than the sum of the individual objects.

The royal tombs of Sipán have provided our first opportunity to accurately reconstruct such an ensemble. Although multiple sets of objects are included in the inventory of each tomb (e.g., three sets of ear ornaments), it is possible to select one of each type, and thus compile a typical complete set of clothing, ornaments, and ritual objects that would have been worn and used together. The Warrior Priest from Tomb 1 might well have been dressed as follows (Fig. 245): he wears a long tunic which is completely covered with square platelets of gilded copper, and has gilded copper cones at the hem. On his wrists are large beaded bracelets of turquoise, shell, and gold. His chest and shoulders are covered with a beaded pectoral of gold and silver beads. Around his waist is a belt which supports crescent-shaped bells and a warrior's backflap, the latter consisting of nearly a kilogram of gold. A crescent-shaped gold nose ornament, suspended from the septum of his nose, completely covers his mouth and the lower part of his face. In his ear lobes he wears large ear ornaments inlaid with gold and turquoise. On his head he wears a large, crescent-shaped headdress ornament of gold, and in one hand he holds a gold and silver scepter, the primary insignia of his rank.

Such a spectacular array of objects, worn by a single individual at one time, seems to us rather ostentatious. Yet in Moche art high status adult males are often depicted in such attire. The royal tombs of Sipán have allowed us to see and examine the actual objects depicted in the art and thus to appreciate their technological sophistication, their artistic beauty, and the amount and variety of precious materials used in their manufacture. The realization that Moche elite dressed with such splendor on ceremonial occasions provides ample testimony to the genius of this ancient civilization — its arts, technology, and extraordinary sense of pageantry.

GOLD-SILVER DUALITY

The royal tombs of Sipán have clearly demonstrated that the Moche deliberately paired gold and silver in a symbolic duality. The simplest expression of this was to string gold and silver beads together on the same necklace. In Tomb 1, for example, we found the necklace of peanut beads consisting of ten gold and ten silver peanuts. The gold beads began over the right shoulder of the wearer and continued to the midpoint of the chest. At that point, they were replaced by silver beads, which continued up over the left shoulder.

Another expression of the gold-silver duality was the practice of making a pair of objects of similar size and form, one of gold and the other of silver. In Tomb 1 there was a gold *tumi* and a silver *tumi* of nearly identical size and form. There were also two warrior backflaps, one of gold and the other of silver. Finally, there was a gold ingot on the individual's right hand and a silver ingot on his left hand. In Tomb 3, there were not only matched pairs of gold and silver backflaps, but also matched pairs of gold and silver bells.

FIG. 246

Excavating the Tomb of the Priestess at San José de Moro.

A third way in which the Moche paired gold and silver was to fabricate objects in halves, one half in gold and the other in silver. The nose ornament and backflap from Tomb 2, for example, have gold and silver in complementary halves.

The pairing of gold and silver is so common that it appears to have had a symbolic meaning to the Moche. It is interesting that it almost always involved exhibiting gold on the proper right side of the individual, and silver on the proper left side. This is consistent with beliefs and practices of the native people of Peru at the time of European contact. Early Colonial Period accounts state that the native people believed in the duality and complementarity of right and left halves. They associated gold with masculinity and the right side, and silver with femininity and the left side. Placement by the Moche of gold on the right and silver on the left strongly suggests that these gender associations were part of their culture too.

THE SACRIFICE CEREMONY

Perhaps the most remarkable aspect of the royal tombs of Sipán is that the objects buried with the principal individuals in Tombs 1 and 2 have allowed us to identify them as specific individuals who participated in the Sacrifice Ceremony. When these individuals were first identified in the Moche Archive at UCLA in 1974, we never imagined that we would some day witness the excavation of their tombs! But doing so clearly demonstrated that the Sacrifice Ceremony was a *real event*, with the principal individuals dressed precisely as they are depicted in the art in order to perform their ceremonial roles.

Moreover, the ritual offerings of amputated hands and feet that we excavated on the south platform strongly imply that the Sacrifice Ceremony was actually performed at or near this pyramid, and that the remains resulting from its enactment were ritually buried in the pyramid itself. For the first time, then, we have been able to make a direct correlation between a ceremonial event depicted in Moche art and the individuals who performed that ceremony, the place where it was enacted, and the disposal of ritual remains after the ceremony was completed.

In 1991, after the three royal tombs at Sipán had been excavated, the tomb of a woman who served as the Priestess at the Sacrifice Ceremony was excavated approximately fifty kilometers south of Sipán (Donnan and Castillo 1992). The tomb was found at San José de Moro, an archaeological site located in the lower Jequetepeque Valley (Fig. 1). It had a room-sized burial chamber, like Tombs 1 and 2 at Sipán, which contained multiple individuals and great quantities of associated grave contents (Fig. 246).

FIG. 247
———
(top) Large
silver plumes
in the Tomb
of the Priestess
at San José
de Moro.

FIG. 248
———
(bottom) Basin
with cups from
the Tomb of
the Priestess
at San José
de Moro.

FIG. 249

Mural from
Pañamarca
showing the
Priestess (left)
and basin with
cups (right).

The woman was buried with a metal goblet the size and form of the one used in the Sacrifice Ceremony, and she had a pair of large plumes made of a silver-copper alloy, which were identical to those that characterize the headdress of the Priestess in the Sacrifice Ceremony (Fig. 247).

In the corner of the tomb was a large blackware ceramic basin containing cups and a tall goblet (Fig. 248). An identical blackware basin with cups is shown associated with the Priestess in a Moche mural at the site of Pañamarca (Fig. 249) in the Nepeña Valley (Fig. 1). Furthermore, the tall goblet in the ceramic basin was of the type used at the Sacrifice Ceremony and was decorated with anthropomorphized clubs and shields holding similar goblets.

How does the tomb at San José de Moro relate to Tombs 1 and 2 from Sipán? First, it should be noted that the two tombs at Sipán date to approximately A.D. 300, and the one at San José de Moro dates to at least 250 years later — sometime after A.D. 550. This demonstrates that the Sacrifice Ceremony had a long duration in Moche culture, with individuals consistently dressing in the same traditional garments, ornaments, and headdresses.

The Sacrifice Ceremony was also widespread geographically. The Pañamarca mural, which clearly depicts this ceremony, was found in the southern part of the Moche kingdom, more than 300 kilometers south of Sipán. Loma Negra, on the other hand, is located on the northern margin of the Moche kingdom, more than 200 kilometers north of Sipán. Perhaps each of the other river valleys that were part of the Moche kingdom also had a central ceremonial precinct where the Sacrifice Ceremony was enacted.

The fact that the Sacrifice Ceremony was so widespread in both time and space strongly implies that it was part of a state religion, with a priesthood in each part of the kingdom composed of nobles who dressed in prescribed ritual attire. When members of the priesthood died, they were buried at the temple where the Sacrifice Ceremony took place, wearing the objects they had used to perform the ritual. Subsequently, other men and women were chosen to replace them, to dress like them, and to perform the same ceremonial role.

Thus the royal tombs of Sipán have given us many important new insights into Moche culture. They provide a much clearer understanding of Moche social organization, which we now realize had a wealthier class of nobles than we had ever imagined. The burial of these nobles with multiple sets of sumptuous clothing and ornaments would have created the need to support many highly skilled artisans to replenish the material that was being removed by royal burial. This, in turn, has helped explain the extraordinary artistic and technological achievements of the Moche, who were truly the mastercraftsmen of ancient America.

The royal tombs of Sipán have also provided important insights about Moche art and Moche religion. The art, we now realize, accurately documented real events enacted by real people. We also now realize that Moche religion involved ceremonial rituals with priests and priestesses dressed in rigidly prescribed paraphernalia. The rituals appear to have been performed for centuries throughout the Moche kingdom without changes in the activities, the priestly roles, or the ritual attire.

Although information derived recently from La Mina and San José de Moro has helped to confirm and refine our understanding of Moche culture, it was the excavations of the royal tombs at Sipán that provided the key. They not only contained the richest treasures ever excavated archaeologically in the Western Hemisphere but also provided valuable information that has fundamentally altered our perception of Moche society.

The contents of the royal tombs of Sipán are wonderful. They provide a dramatic contrast to the contents of the looted tomb, the remains of which are now divided and scattered in private collections throughout the world, unavailable for scholarly research or public viewing. Instead, the contents of these excavated tombs will be kept together, available for people today and in the future to see and appreciate.

Although the treasures found in these wondrous tombs seem priceless, of perhaps greater value is the extraordinary new cultural information that they provide, information that is helping us formulate a much clearer and more accurate reconstruction of the Moche — one of the most remarkable civilizations of the ancient world.

BIBLIOGRAPHY

Arriaga, Pablo José de
1968   The Extirpation of Idolotry in Peru. University of Kentucky Press, Lexington.

Cordy-Collins, Alana
1992   Archaism or Continuing Tradition: The Decapitator Theme in Cupisnique and
        Moche Iconography. Latin American Antiquity. Vol. 3(3):206-220.

Donnan, Christopher B.
1978   Moche Art of Peru. Museum of Cultural History, University of California, Los Angeles.
1982   La Caza del Venado en el Arte Mochica. Revista del Museo Nacional. Tomo XLVI. Lima.

Donnan, Christopher B., and Luis Jaime Castillo
1992   Finding the Tomb of a Moche Priestess. Archaeology. Vol. 45(6):38-42.

Kutscher, Gerdt
1954   Nordperuanische Keramik. Casa Editoria, Gebr. Mann. Berlin.

Lechtman, Heather, Antonieta Erly, and Edward J. Barry, Jr.
1982   New Perspectives on Moche Metallurgy: Techniques of Gilding Copper at Loma Negra,
        Northern Peru. American Antiquity. Vol. 47(1):3-30.

McClelland, Donna
1977   The Ulluchu: A Moche Symbolic Fruit. In Pre-Columbian Art History: Selected Readings,
        A. Cordy-Collins and J. Stern (eds.), pp. 435-452. Peek Publications, Palo Alto.

Ubbelohde-Doering, Heinrich
1983   Vorspanische Gräber von Pacatnamú, Nordperu. Materialien zur Allgemeinen und
        Vergleichenden Archäologie Band 26. Verlag C.H. Beck, München.

Verano, John W.
1990   The Moche: Profile of an Ancient Peruvian People. Anthropology Notes. Vol. 12(1):1-15.
ms.a   Physical Characteristics and Skeletal Biology of the Moche Population at Pacatnamu.
        Manuscript on file, Fowler Museum of Cultural History, University of California,
        Los Angeles.
ms.b   Human Skeletal Remains from Sipán. Manuscript on file, Fowler Museum of Cultural
        History, University of California, Los Angeles.

Wassén, Henry
1985/86 Ulluchu in Moche Iconography and Blood Ceremonies: the Search for Identification.
         Etnografiska Museum Arstryck Annals, pp. 59-85. Göteborg.

CREDITS

Source of Illustrations
▼

All photographs by Christopher Donnan unless otherwise noted. All objects are property of the Museo Nacional Bruning, Lambayeque, Perú, unless otherwise noted.

Front and back covers. Photographs by Susan Einstein.
Page 10. Photograph by Bill Ballenberg.
Figure 1. Map by Donald McClelland.
3. Collection of Jaclyn and Sydney J. Rosenberg.
4. Collection of Dr. and Mrs. Franklin Murphy. Photograph by Denis Nervig.
5. Fowler Museum of Cultural History, UCLA.
6, 7. Fowler Museum of Cultural History, UCLA. Photographs by Denis Nervig.
8. Art Institute of Chicago. Photograph by Robert Hashimoto. Buckingham Fund, 1955.2338.
9. Linden Museum Stuttgart.
10. Fowler Museum of Cultural History, UCLA. Photograph by Denis Nervig.
11. Drawing by Donna McClelland.
12. Private Collection.
13. Museo Nacional de Antropología, Arqueología e Historia del Perú, Lima.
14. Phoebe Apperson Hearst Museum, University of California Berkeley.
15. Private Collection. Photograph by Denis Nervig.
16 a, b. Private Collection.
17. Fowler Museum of Cultural History, UCLA. Photograph by Denis Nervig.
18. Map by Donald McClelland.
19. Photographic Archives, Bruning Museum.
23. Photograph by Susan Einstein.
24, 25. Photographs by Christopher Donnan and Donald McClelland.
32. Collection of Hernán Miranda.
34. Photograph by Christopher Donnan and Donald McClelland.
35. Private Collection.
36. Photograph by Christopher Donnan and Donald McClelland.
38. Photograph by Bill Ballenberg.
39. Painting by Alberto Gutiérrez. Photograph by Guillermo Hare.
40. Drawing by Alberto Gutiérrez.
44. Photograph by Christopher Donnan and Donald McClelland.
47. Photograph by Martha Cooper.
49. Photograph by Donald McClelland.
50, 51. Photographs by Bill Ballenberg.
52. Photograph by Guillermo Cock.
53. Photographic Archives, Bruning Museum.
54, 55. Photographic Archives, Bruning Museum.
56. Photograph by Guillermo Cock.
57. Painting by Ned Seidler.
63. Drawing by Donna McClelland.
66. Photograph by Susan Einstein.
67. Drawing by Donna McClelland.
68. Private Collection.
69. Drawing by Alberto Gutiérrez.
70, 71, 72, 73. Photographic Archives, Bruning Museum.
74. Photograph by Susan Einstein.
75. Photograph by Donald McClelland.
76. Photograph by Christopher Donnan and Donald McClelland.
77. Photographic Archives, Bruning Museum.
79, 80, 81, 84. Photographs by Donald McClelland.
85. Photograph by Susan Einstein.
86. Photograph by Donald McClelland.
87. Photograph by Susan Einstein.
89, 91. Photographic Archives, Bruning Museum.
93. Drawing by Donna McClelland.

94. Photographic Archives, Bruning Museum.
96. Photograph by Susan Einstein.
99. Photograph by Denis Nervig.
101. Photographic Archives, Bruning Museum.
115 a, b. Photographs by John Verano.
116, 117, 118, 120. Photographic Archives, Bruning Museum.
121. Photograph by Christopher Donnan and Donald McClelland.
126. Drawing by Donna McClelland.
128. Photographic Archives, Bruning Museum.
130. Photograph by Bill Ballenberg.
133. Drawing by Alberto Gutiérrez.
134. Painting by Percy Fiestas. Photograph by Guillermo Hare.
135. Fowler Museum of Cultural History, UCLA. Photograph by Denis Nervig.
136, 137, 138. Drawings by Donna McClelland.
139. Drawing by Robert Easley.
140. Drawing by Donna McClelland.
141. After Kutscher 1954:23.
142, 143. Drawings by Donna McClelland.
144. After Kutscher 1954:25B.
145, 146. Drawings by Donna McClelland.
147. The Metropolitan Museum of Art. Photograph by The Metropolitan Museum of Art.
148. The Metropolitan Museum of Art. Photograph by Robert Woolard.
149. The Art Institute of Chicago. Photograph by Robert Woolard.
150. Peabody Museum, Harvard University, Cambridge. Photograph by Susan Einstein.
151. Collection of Jaclyn and Sydney J. Rosenberg. Photograph by Robert Woolard.
152. Drawing by Donna McClelland.
153. Private Collection.
157. Painting by Percy Fiestas. Photograph by Susan Einstein.
161. Drawing by Donna McClelland.
167, 168. Photographic Archives, Bruning Museum.
169, 171, 173. Drawings by Alberto Gutiérrez.
174. Painting by Percy Fiestas. Photograph by Guillermo Hare.
175, 176, 177, 180. Photographic Archives, Bruning Museum.
181. Photograph by Guillermo Cock.
182. Photographic Archives, Bruning Museum.
183. Painting by Percy Fiestas. Photograph by Guillermo Hare.
184. Photograph by Christopher Donnan and Donald McClelland.
185. Drawing by Alberto Gutiérrez.
186. Photograph by Christopher Donnan and Donald McClelland.
187. Photographic Archives, Bruning Museum.
188. Drawing by Alberto Gutiérrez.
189, 191, 192. Photographic Archives, Bruning Museum.
193. Drawing by Alberto Gutiérrez.
195. Photograph by Christopher Donnan and Donald McClelland.
196. Photographic Archives, Bruning Museum.
198. Painting by Tom Hall.
199. Drawing by Alberto Gutiérrez.
201. Drawing by Donna McClelland.
202. Photograph by Guillermo Cock.
204. Photograph by Susan Einstein.
205, 208. Photographic Archives, Bruning Museum.
209. Painting by Alberto Gutiérrez. Photograph by Guillermo Hare.
210, 211. Photographs by Guillermo Cock.
212. Photograph by Christopher Donnan and Donald McClelland.
214. Photographic Archives, Bruning Museum.
216. Photograph by Guillermo Cock.
217, 218, 221, 222, 223, 224, 225, 228, 229, 230. Photographs by Christopher Donnan and Donald McClelland.
234, 235, 236, 239, 240, 241, 242, 243, 244. Photographic Archives, Bruning Museum.
245. Photograph by Susan Einstein.
246, 247. Photographs by Donald McClelland.
249. Painting by Felix Caycho. © Gonzalo de Reparaz.

Publication Presentation

▼

UCLA PRINT COMMUNICATIONS

Judy Hale
Production
Coordination

Barbara Kelly
Design

▼

FOWLER MUSEUM OF CULTURAL HISTORY

Daniel R. Brauer
Director of
Publications

Anthony A.G. Kluck
Assistant to
the Director of
Publications

▼

Editing and layout were accomplished on Macintosh computers using QuarkXPress and Adobe Stone Sans, Stone Serif and Charlemagne font software.